## Praise For The Book

Own It: Redefining Responsibility is a must read for anyone looking for an innovative approach to the challenge of employee engagement. In this powerful work, Meridith reveals how this economy has changed, why engaging today's employees is different, and specifically what you need to do build a team that is as passionate about your organization as you are. This book needs to be on the reading list of any leader who is looking for cutting edge ideas on how to build and attract top talent in the new economy.

*Diana Oreck*
*Vice President Ritz-Carlton Leadership Center*

"Meridith Elliott Powell has done it again! Just when you didn't think that she could top her latest bestselling book "Winning In The Trust & Value Economy", Meridith hits a home run with "Own It: Redefining Responsibility "!Gallup has reported that 70%+ of today's employees have just checked out! "Own It: Redefining Responsibility" is a practical how-to book for professionals and business managers that want to master the skill of employee engagement. If you manage any employees or just want to know why you're not "engaged" in your own job, you need to read "Own It: Redefining Responsibility"!

*Lon Safko, author of the $2m Bestselling book*
*"The Social Media Bible" & "The Fusion Marketing Bible"*

Meridith Elliott Powell has done it again! *Own It: Redefining Responsibility* is truly exceptional because it reveals a surprising truth...that employee engagement is *everybody's* responsibility, not just management's. Meridith shares practical, effective practices and principles both for leadership to develop the engaged culture and for employees to own their crucial roles in developing unstoppable teams. *Own It: Redefining Responsibility* will inspire readers to collaborate and win the engagement challenge!

*Brian Biro*
*America's Breakthrough Coach*
*Author of 11 books including Beyond Success*

"Leave it to Meridith to find an innovative and powerful way to tackle the number one issue facing leaders today – employee engagement! In **Own It: Redefining Responsibility**, Meridith clearly defines why current employee engagement solutions are not working. Then she provides you with  cutting edge strategies and techniques that can easily take your team and your company to a whole new level. Looking for a book that will give you competitive advantage  – **Own It: Redefining Responsibility** if the book you need!"

*Jack Hubbard*
*Chairman & Chief Sales Officer*
*St Meyer & Hubbard*

"Meridith's new book is a must read for anyone who hires people. If we keep doing what we've been doing, we won't necessarily keep getting what we've been getting. Generations have dramatically changed, people want different things now out of their jobs than ever before, and what worked once for finding and retaining tremendously talented people no longer works. With so many distractions and ways in which we can spend our time, not to mention the stresses of life that seem to be bigger than ever, it is easy to disengage while at work. **Own It**: Redefining Responsibility is a practical, easy to follow, and enlightening guide to not just finding the best people out there, but more importantly motivating them and keeping them passionate and excited about their jobs, your company, and their future. Meridith is a master at teaching us how to bring out the best in people, and turning them into cheerleaders for your organization."

*Ed Hart*
*Director, Center for Family Business*
*Cal State University, Fullerton*
*President, Hart Professional Services*

# OWN IT

## Redefining Responsibility

**Stories of Power, Freedom & Purpose**

Meridith Elliott Powell

Published by Motivational Press, Inc.
1777 Aurora Road
Melbourne, Florida, 32935

www.MotivationalPress.com

Manufactured in the United States of America.

ISBN:  978-1-62865-272-7

# CONTENTS

# ACKNOWLEDGMENTS

Own It: Redefining Responsibility is a book I have wanted to write ever since I discovered how powerful taking ownership of your life and your career can be. From that point on, it became a passion of mine to help people, in both their personal and their professional lives, understand just how freeing and liberating taking responsibility can be.

Lucky for me, I discovered early on that this is a passion and a message I share with so many. As I began the process of researching and writing the book, I was blown away by the number of people I met who were as committed to spreading the word as I am. It is those people that so openly shared their stories that I want to thank, and those individuals to whom I want to both acknowledge and dedicate this book.

My Clients – over the years I discovered that my favorite clients, those whom later would become my "niche," were those leaders that wasted no time complaining. Instead they were the type of people who looked first to themselves for the answers, the ideas and the solutions to take their companies and their teams to the next level. It is this group that I think for the many stories and ideas that are a part of this book.

My Husband – a true self-made man and success, it is my husband's drive and relentless commitment that keeps me motivated and inspired.

My Family – we have been through so much, and found that the path to recovery could only be found through personal responsibly.

My Friends – who are always there for me, keep me from getting lonely on the road, and provide me unconditional support and love

My Future Connections – so looking forward to where this book takes me, and who it connects me to. Feeling confident that my future will lead me to interesting people that are as passionate about personal responsibility as I am.

Again, I want to thank all of the people in my life, present and future, that have motivated and inspired me on my journey to spread the word about responsibility. In my opinion, responsibility is powerful tool to "cure" what is wrong with so many areas of our professional and personal lives, and my hope is that by reading this book you will join me on this journey!

# INTRODUCTION

I am on a mission! I want to share an important piece of information that is critical for success both professionally and personally. It is an important piece of information, that for some reason, is rarely talked about, and even more rarely embraced. However, it is such a powerful piece of information that when put into action, it can have a direct impact on both the level of success you achieve and the ease as to which you get there. This important piece of information is responsibility, personal responsibility. A common word for such a powerful force, as responsibility is the very "thing" that can, in a moment, turn you from being driven by change to driving it, and take you from struggle to the position of control.

So you see, my mission is to share the word about this important skill, and bring personal responsibility back into the workplace. I want to redefine how we perceive it and its impact on our careers and our lives. In the last few years, I feel that my business has transformed from that of a speaker, coach, and consultant to a leadership professional who has found her calling. In turn, this calling has resulted in my joining or initiating (I am not quite sure which) this movement to redefine what it means to be a responsible human in the present-day workforce. My aim is also to transform the concept of personal responsibility from an association with feeling burdened and overwhelmed, to a concept that implies taking control of your life and experiencing a greater overall level of freedom, passion and power. In other words, I want to foster a movement that embraces taking "personal responsibility" and that gives professionals (employees and business leaders) the ability to take charge of their careers and achieve greater success in life. In my opinion, our current beliefs about responsibility and entitlement are the root of what is wrong with our employee engagement programs and why they are failing, miserably.

Why do I care, and why am I so passionate about workplace responsibility? It is because I believe taking personal responsibility is the key to putting you in the driver's seat, whether it is your business, your leadership role, or your own career , personal responsibility is what is going to put you in charge of you. Embracing responsibility is the great equalizer; meaning that no matter your position in a company, whether you are at the beginning of your career or on the verge of retiring; whether you are part of a Fortune 100 company or running your own small business, personal responsibility creates the capacity for success to be determined by you, rather than by someone else. I believe the current economy in the United States, while challenging and shifting, is still one in which you can be successful. My goal is to help you believe that too, and help you learn how you can take your career and your life to a completely new level.

My exploration into the meaning of personal responsibility started after I wrote the book Winning in the Trust & Value Economy: A Guide To Business & Sales Success. That was a book I wrote as a response to the overwhelming array of challenges professionals and business owners faced in 2008 due to the global economic recession. In 2008, my clients and followers were struggling with the negative economy, trying to figure out how to navigate this challenging economy and what specifically they needed to do to stay afloat, let alone grow their businesses. By 2014, their concern had moved beyond business growth to the challenges of workplace dysfunction and the issue of attracting and retaining talented employees. Whenever I engaged with CEOs or C-Suite professionals, they would share their biggest challenge seemed to be attracting and retaining "talent." Meanwhile, employees were expressing their frustrations with being overwhelmed with too much work to do, tired of being asked to do more with less, and tired of being afraid they would lose their jobs in the next round of layoffs. The combination of which reduced their ability to work effectively and efficiently.

Similar to my investigation of the impact of business growth strategies on the economy and on professionals in Winning in the Trust & Value Economy I began to investigate why our current employee engagement strategies no longer appeared to be working. "We" were spending more money than ever before on programs and workplace perks in an effort to solve the employee engagement problem, yet the problem kept getting worse. In interviews and conversations, professionals and leaders were sharing their frustration that the retention strategies they were currently using were just not effective anymore. Instead, they were producing a higher degree of fear in employees, and limiting the ability of companies to attract and retain top talent. So my curiosity got the best of me; I wanted to know why our current strategies were not working, and I wanted to discover what strategies would work in the current climate, and what methods were best to effectively implement them. The economy, the workforce competition, and even the clients/customers have changed since the end of the recession that began in 2008. So it made sense to me, it seemed natural to me, that new strategies and a new way of thinking would be needed to solve today's employee and leadership challenges.

I got my first clue to this puzzle on, of all places, a golf trip to Jupiter, Florida. I was playing Jupiter Hills Country Club with a friend, and before heading out on the back nine, we went in to grab a quick lunch. Just as we were finishing, her husband and three of his buddies came over to join us. Now, all four of these men are highly successful, multi-millionaires several times over, and the very definition of the American Dream. All four of these men, including my friend's husband, grew up by today's standards poor, very poor, yet despite having the odds stacked against them all had managed to achieve, by anyone's measure, extreme success. I thought about that, as I listened to them tell jokes and stories, and I began to wonder how they got here, and what it took, what was the secret to that level of success.

I found it amazing (and wanted to know) how someone could go from living in the poorest of neighborhoods to living in the most exclusive neighborhoods, or how someone could begin their life on the receiving end of charity and later become powerfully philanthropic, or how someone could begin their adult working life hoping to just find a job and subsequently become the employer of thousands of people. This did not just happen, it was not just a lucky break, I was sure there was more to it. I wanted to know, what these men had done that enabled them to advance so far toward their goals.

I wanted to know, so I asked, and their generosity of time, and their honest and engaging stories helped me understand and shaped my perspective for this book, and about the power of personal responsibility. These four men showed me why personal responsibility is not a burden but a path to power, freedom, and purpose. Their "ownership" of their success is what sparked my realization that our current ideas regarding employee engagement, leadership and career success are outdated and ineffective. Listening to these men also taught me that to create cultures of employee engagement, leaders and employees need to work together, and in doing so will inspire ownership at every level and enhance profits at every turn.

Needless to say, after one afternoon (which stretched into a weekend) with these men, I was inspired and encouraged, and I knew I had a message that was important for both leaders and employees. The following chapters paint the picture and provide the statistics and research of what is not working with our current engagement programs, what will work, and the amazing stories of companies and individuals who have joined the movement and are redefining responsibility into their personal journey of success.

Why should you read this book? By reading the following chapters, you will learn why measuring success today differs from that a decade ago; why the level of engagement of each and every member of your team is your hedge against your competition; and how you can make the necessary changes to make this economy start working for you. More importantly, in this fun and easy read you will learn how to foster that workplace culture that inspires "personal responsibility" and/or how to become the employee that companies strive to keep during difficult economic times!

This book is written in three parts. Each one builds on the next, and, taken as a whole, these can help you create an employee engagement program that includes efforts from the employees in leadership roles to the employees throughout every level of your organization.

Part I describes how the economy has changed, how those changes are impacting your clients and customers, and how those changes are impacting you as a leader or team member. This section also guides you on how to adapt to the changed economy in order to succeed in it.

It is in this section that the current state of employee engagement is described in depth. This section examines why employee engagement is at an all-time low, and why our current attempts to address the issue are not working. Here, you will be introduced to traditional approaches to employee engagement, the reasons why these are not working (and why you need to change them), and the foundational shift that needs to be implemented to ensure your teams of employees are ready to step up to the plate, take ownership of their work, and drive successful results.

You'll finish this section actually feeling better, like when you realize you have been doing something the hard way, and someone comes along, makes a minor adjustment, and miraculously makes your job a whole lot easier.

Part II is aimed at leaders or business owners, but I encourage any and all to still invest the time in reading this section. Part II is written for those who are in charge of attracting, developing, and retaining talent. Even if you are not a leader, this part can help you better understand how to recognize and differentiate an engaging work culture. You will be able to clearly differentiate an engaging culture from one that is not engaging.

This part will show business and organizational leaders the fundamental shift in today's employees, and the reason why engaging them now is so different from the past. In this section, we will help you understand the employee perspective and how by understanding it you can tap into their intrinsic motivation. The section guides you through building a culture that inspires and encourages motivation and personal responsibility. Chock full of specific strategies, real-life examples, and techniques, this section shifts your paradigm and creates a very different view of how to engage employees. It specifically focuses on how your role as a leader has changed, and provides an action plan, a step-by-step guide of how to build a culture of what I like to call "employee innovation."

Part III is for the employee (and again, while it is designed specifically for those wanting to be hired by and retained in a company, I encourage anyone to read it, and specifically leaders and business owners) and sets the stage for how you become the employee that companies strive to keep. Again, if you are a leader or an employee, then this section is also for you. The better you understand what those employees that want to engage are doing and thinking, the better you will be able to create cultures that engage them.

Instead of focusing on the leader creating a culture of employee engagement, this part zeros in on the employees' experiences and engagement-related activities. Taking an innovative approach to employee engagement, Part III empowers you, as an employee, to create a culture of employee engagement, giving you the tools, skills, and strategy to understand how to step up to the plate, take ownership, and drive results. This section guides you through a series of stories, real-life examples, and techniques that help you understand why and how engaging is of benefit to you, and how to do it whether the culture you work in invites it or not.

Throughout this book, you will find one of my favorite sections, "In Their Own Words." This section will be highlighted in a box and will offer insights into the strategy or rule we are discussing, while using personal experience and real-life stories that show us how easy and effective it is to implement these ideas. In addition, this book has case studies and client stories to bring key points to life. Each chapter ends with a next-steps section entitled "Call to Action." "Calls to Action" give you an exact plan and strategy to put what you just learned into action and to ensure your return on investment.

So sit back, relax, and enjoy a great read that will not only be fun but that will provide powerful information to help you understand your capacity to affect changes in employee engagement. Be able to produce positive results by embracing the idea of personal responsibility, which will put you in charge of your own success!

# PART I

## THE FOUNDATION - UNDERSTANDING THE STATE OF EMPLOYEE ENGAGEMENT

# CHAPTER 1

## A NEW ECONOMY CALLS FOR A NEW APPROACH

n March of 2009, I was in Charlotte, North Carolina in a meeting with my peers and colleagues. We were all there to hear a sales guru, a true master in the art, who was presenting a program about how to take your businesses and your career to the next level.

This guru began his talk that day by asking us, "Who in here is struggling in this economy, who is challenged by this down economy?" Now, you have to remember, this is 2009, and we are just starting to feel the impact of this economic downturn. In addition, we are all colleagues and peers, so there is no way we are going to admit in front of one another that we are having any trouble, let alone struggling. Being a master speaker and business expert, our guru senses our hesitation and begins to relax his voice. He begins talking in this soothing tone; the more he speaks, the more he draws us in like moths to a flame, until most of us are waving our hands in the air saying, "AMEN, Brother, it is tough out there. I am a victim."

About that time, our guru asks his second question: "Is anyone in this room doing really well in this economy, having a good year, having a great year?" Then, three individuals proudly start waving their hands in the air. The rest of us are starting to sense we have definitely walked into something! Now, our guru asks his third question: "Okay, so if some of you are struggling in this economy, if some of you are rockin' it off the chart, I just have to wonder: Do you think it is the economy or YOU that is standing in the way of your own success?"

The moment that rolled off his tongue, I thought, "OUCH that hurt," and I realized I had walked right into his trap. Then I quickly started making excuses for myself: "He doesn't get it, he doesn't understand how difficult things are out there, how tough it is to compete in my world, or even just how tough it is to be me." Then, thank goodness, I thought, "As much as I hate to admit it, that is a good question, good, but painful. I mean, truly, if others are doing well in this economy, if some people are having a really great year, and I am not, maybe it is me and not the economy that is standing in the way of my own success."

That was my paradigm shift, that was my big "Ah Ha" moment, and it came in 2009 on that day, in that meeting, with that guru. That was when I realized that I was not taking responsibility for my success. Instead, even without realizing it, I was "blaming" my clients, the economy, and even my employees and my competition. I was looking outside myself for the reasons I was struggling or challenged, when the truth was I had everything I needed to succeed. Everything, I just was not pushing myself, not doing anything differently than I had done in the past, and I certainly was not taking the initiative to figure out what others were doing to be successful in this economy and to learn from their strategies.

So yes, things are tough, just not as easy as they used to be. What is going on, what has changed? Welcome to the new economy, where the only thing that is certain is uncertainty. To truly understand how to build a culture where employees are fully engaged (or how to become the employee that companies strive to keep), you need to start there, with understanding our new economic reality.

No matter what our reporters or politicians say, this economy is not down or up, what it is is changed, radically different. So different that things are never, I mean never, going back to the way that they were. In fact, economists agree, and they say that we have literally gone through an economic shift, moving out of what is known as a "push" economy and into what is called a "pull" economy. While there is a lot to know and understand about this shift, all you really need to know as leaders, team members, and business owners, is that when we made this shift, the consumer, your customers, moved into the position of control. They are holding all the cards, and have the power to make the decisions about when, from where and whom they buy. Think about it; think about how much change has happened in our economy in the last five to ten years: globalization, constant advancements in technology, and increasing competition. The truth is, we could all get up right now, go home, and sit around in our PJS, our sweatpants or heck we could even sit around in our underwear for the next weeks if we wanted to, and Google until our hearts are content researching, learning and buying whatever it is we want.

Just take a moment and think about that. We can buy groceries, office supplies, and even a new car, all online. We can join groups, attend networking events, support our favorite charities, heck, we can even make a friend, get a date, get married, and get divorced! We can do all of that without ever having to take a bath, get dressed, utter a phrase, or leave the comfort of our own home ever again.

That right there, that changes EVERYTHING! This is an economy like no other, an economy like none we have ever lived in, worked in, developed a team in, let alone had to grow a business in before. It's no wonder the rules of how we grow a company and how we engage employees need to change, the economy has changed, and to succeed we need to change with it.

In today's economy, with the increases in competition and the availability of technology and the Internet, the products and services we sell have become a commodity. Consumers believe, and they are right, they can buy them anywhere, with a click of a Mouse. This is a global economy, where consumers can choose to buy products or services in their hometown, three states away, or anywhere in the world. So, I know you think your business, your store is unique or special, but no matter how unique you believe your product or service is, to the consumer, your customer, it has become a commodity. So, in the new economy, the products or services we offer are not the true reason our customers are buying from us, the true reason is how we offer it, how we position it, is. That is now our competitive advantage.

In today's economy, trust is what attracts the customer to you, and value is what keeps them long term! That is why in my last book, Winning in the Trust & Value Economy, I gave this new economy a name, the Trust & Value Economy. This is a relationship economy, a relationship economy that is as much about the relationships that you build with your employees as it is about the ones you build with our customers. In fact, I believe that in this economy, the relationships that you build with your employees are more important to the success of your company than the relationships you build with your customers.

Why? Because in this economy, it is not the product or service you are selling—it is the experience your customers are having. In today's new economy, that is what is growing your business, and that is what is transferring to your bottom line. Now think about it: The experience your customers are having is dependent upon the level of engagement of your employees..

Creating an amazing customer experience would all be so easy if you—the owner, leader, CEO—were the only one interacting with your customers, but you are not. Not only are you not the only one interacting with your customers, but your employees are most likely having more interaction with your customers than you. Kind of scary when you think about it, isn't it? You need your employees to be fully engaged, to care as much about your customers' experience as you do.

## THE REAL WORLD

*As a business owner, you have to wonder how much a disengaged employee and the word "NO" are costing you. A few months ago, my husband and I had some friends suffer some tragic news, feeling helpless and in an effort to provide some comfort we did what all friends do, we offered to bring food!*

*With no time to cook or prepare a meal, both my husband and I decided to make some calls to find out where we could order some great, healthy food to just pick up and deliver. The first place I called was a local, small restaurant that prepared daily dinner take-outs, casseroles, and catering. Since I needed an order for about ten, they suggested I take advantage of their daily "family" dinner special, which could easily be ready for pick-up by 5:30 p.m. the next day. Happy with the suggestion and thrilled with the menu, I placed the order.*

*Later that evening, we called to see how our neighbors were doing. Relieved that their spirits were high and their children were with them, we shared that we would see them the next night with dinner and some snacks. They thanked us for the gesture and support, but asked that we not bring too much, as their appetites were low and eating was not high on their list.*

*So the next morning, I called to explain the situation to the restaurant and asked to reduce our order from ten to six. The friendly woman who answered the phone listened and said that she understood but that, unfortunately, their policy stated they "require" a minimum of ten for catering and could no longer fill our order. Disappointed and a little confused as to why a business would turn down a paying customer without even suggesting alternatives, I thanked her for her time and started to make some other calls.*

*My next call was to a healthy grocery store in town, the kind of place that sells all kinds of healthy and organic products and always has an amazing deli section filled with wonderfully pre-prepared meats and vegetables. You know the type of place you can run into and grab enough great food to put on an amazing dinner party at the last minute.*

*Again, a very friendly woman answered the phone and shared that she would love to help me, but that their policy is they "required" twenty-four hours' notice. One more time, I thanked her and hung up the phone a little confused. This time I had to laugh and thought to myself, "You need twenty-four hours to put six pieces of chicken and some rice and vegetables in a to-go box?" Remember, this is food they already have laid out in a display case—food that if I came in and ordered at the counter, they would quickly put together with no problem.*

*Finally, I called a local restaurant that my husband and I eat at frequently, I hesitated to call because I know they rarely do to-go orders and do not cater. I explained our situation and said that I needed some help. The friendly woman who answered the phone said she could assist me. She was sure they could put some things together and have it all ready for me by five that afternoon. In addition, she asked if it would be all right if they put it in a basket rather than a box, as it would present so much better to our friends. I thanked her and immediately called my husband to let him know I finally had the situation handled and to tell him the story. I also went to social media, telling hundreds of my "closest friends" about how helpful this restaurant was and, oh yes, how unhelpful the others had been.*

*At five p.m., when I went to pick up the order, they not only had placed it in a lovely basket, but the employees had all signed a get-well card for our friend with kind notes of encouragement. I was thrilled with this restaurant, the food, and the entire experience.*

*And yes while I shared the story with my husband, I was also taking photos, posting them online, and telling all of my "closest friends" how amazing this restaurant was.*

*The very next day, my husband decided to take his entire staff to lunch, and where do you think he went? Of course, to our "helpful" restaurant—the one that, despite not serving dinner and not being a caterer, stepped in and went above and beyond.*

*So, you have to ask yourself: How much is "NO" costing you? How much business are you losing because your employees are not engaged? I feel confident that with any of those businesses, had I had the owner on the phone, had they been the one helping me, there would have been no word of policy or requirements.*

*In this economy you are dependent upon how engaged your employees are; in fact, employee engagement is your key to success in this economy. Ironically, at a time when we need our employees to be fully engaged, we are suffering from the most disengaged workforce in recent history. At a time when customers are demanding more from us, our employees are giving less.*

*$450 billion – That is the number recently released by Gallup, estimating that this disengaged workforce is costing U.S. companies more than $450 billion per year.*

*$700 million – That is the amount U.S. companies are spending annually to try and solve the problem. And according to Bersin & Associates, that number is expected to rise to $1.53 billion in the next few years.*

*70% – That is the number, despite all this money being spent and all these resources committed, of employees admitting to being checked out, unmotivated, and disengaged. And according to the Harvard Business Review, that number is expected to rise to 84% within the next few years.*

So I would say, Houston, we have a problem.

We need our employees to be more engaged than ever, and we are spending more money than ever trying to engage our employees, yet the problem continues to get worse—costing more money and more resources, and getting fewer results. It makes you ask, "Why?"

The good news is, as leaders, we know we have a problem, and we are trying hard to solve it. But when you look at the research, when you see the statistics, don't you wonder why? Why if the approach we are using to solve the problem is not working, why do we we keep using the same, traditional approach?

It is clear from the statistics and the pending upward trend that it is time to turn our approach to both this economy and employee engagement on its head, and create a new style of leadership, one that inspires innovation and growth. A new style of leadership that encourages your team to OWN IT and gets your employees, your leaders, and this economy to start working for you!

---

### CALL TO ACTION SO YOU'RE READY
### YOUR FIRST CALL TO ACTION:

1. *Understand & Embrace – Start here by really spending some time thinking and talking about the fact that this economy is not down, but different. Spend some time as a team, create a task force, or work with your peers and fellow leader to discuss how this economy has changed, and how that change has impacted your experience, your customers' experiences, and your employees.*

2. *Redesign the Path – We are conditioned, as leaders and business owners, to focus on the customer experience and the building of customer relationships. In this step*

*we challenge you to redesign the path, to think about creating a better customer experience by first creating a better employee experience. Again, working with your team or peers, and take some time to trace the current path of the customer experience, recognizing whom they interact with, and who has the greatest impact on their overall experience.*

3. *Trade Control for Uncertainty – Understand that in this economy you are not in control; you need great customers and great employees much more than they need you. Letting go of that control is the first step in understanding the importance of focusing on relationships and experiences with both your customers and your employees.*

# CHAPTER 2

## THE NEW EMPLOYEE: WHAT IS WRONG WITH THIS YOUNGER GENERATION

I remember growing up listening to my father, a small business owner, talk (okay complain) about this "younger generation": how their hair was too long, their music too loud, and how their lack of work ethic was going to ruin this country. Well, while not much has changed over time in terms of the older generation complaining about today's younger workers, the descriptions, goals, and motivations of this workforce certainly have.

In today's marketplace, so much more than the economy has changed: Society, consumers, and competition have been altered, and all of that has impacted and changed your employees. If your goal is to attract, develop, and retain today's best and brightest, then you need to begin by understanding today's employees, no matter their age or their generation.

Today's employees, just like those who have gone before, are smart and innovative; but unlike their predecessors, the economic environment and business culture they are working in are, at best, unstable and in a constant state of change. They have seen and experienced a culture full of disloyalty and broken promises. The world we live in today is very different from the one our parents and grandparents grew up in. And while many things are wonderful about it (technology, travel, diversity, etc.), many things are not, and it is those changes that have greatly shaped today's highly talented but highly skeptical employee.

In the last few decades, we have seen governments rack up debt, others completely default, political scandals become the norm, disgraced CEOS get huge golden parachutes, layoffs and business closures increase, and "too big to fail" well, fail. All of this has greatly impacted our society's ability to trust, shattered our belief in authority, and made us question the payoff of being loyal. To understand today's employees, you need to begin there, because it is much of the reason employees feel less committed and less loyal to employers and corporations.

Building trust today is difficult, and needs to be done slowly and coupled with action and social proof. Now, you can make the argument that your company is trustworthy, or that you as a leader are open and honest with employees. For the most part, you may be right, but honestly, it does not matter, because until employees see it and feel it, trust just does not exist. To really grasp how to fully engage employees, you need to begin by understanding them and the logic of their mistrust. Begin there, then take a long, hard, and honest look at yourself and your company. You need to realize that what you are currently doing to engage your employees, even if you are successful, is probably not going to be enough going forward.

And the reality is, for the most part, today's employees no longer believe they can have, or that they even want, a long-term career with a company. They are no longer looking for a place to retire; instead, they are looking for a job, a very different type of job. As leaders, we need to understand that with stability and the promise of a pension off the table, today's employees are looking for something more to take that place. As employers, we can no longer offer anyone a job for life, a solid retirement, or a guarantee that our companies will not merge or be sold, so understandably, employees want something else, something different. They want their companies to stand for something, and leadership that is driven to make a difference. Employees want their work to matter, and they want a job and an organization they can believe in.

Now you, as a leader, may think, "That is not all that different from what any of us wanted out of our jobs when we began our careers," and you would be right. However, with no trust in long-term employment, this "new employee" has placed a much higher value on purpose and ability to learn and grow. In years past, stock options, pensions, or even great benefit plans could convince an employee to forgo job satisfaction and fulfillment. Today, with those options not part of the conversation, employees want something in exhange: the ability to have a voice in their roles, to do work that matters, and to feel fulfilled by their roles. I would argue that when employers learn how to deliver that, they would not only have a stable workforce, but a fully engaged one.

In this author's opinion, leaders are facing a very different landscape and a very different type of employee when trying to build a workforce today. While, yes, we have the most diverse and multi-generational workforce in history (Traditionalists, Baby Boomers, Generation Xers, and Millennials), all of your workers want the same thing: to be part of something bigger and to do work that matters..

But while all the generations may want the same thing, they are somewhat different in their life perspective, experience, and expectations. We are shaped by the generation we grew up in, what was happening and expected in society at that time, and the social norms of success, family, and education. As leaders, it is important to get a closer look at each generation and their views on work ethic, career, and loyalty.

Who is today's employee? Following is a description of each generation, based on research done by Super Performance Solutions (http://www.super-solutions.com/) and their expertise and work on this topic.

According to Super Performance Solutions, we have four generations actively participating in the workforce today (Traditionalists, Baby Boomers, Gen X and Millennials), more than we have ever had working together before.

## THE TRADITIONALISTS

Born before 1946, there are not too many still in the workforce, but the few that are left are a powerful force to be reckoned with. Traditionalists have a very strong work ethic, a respect for authority, and a strong sense of loyalty. Many have served in the military or been married to someone who has. As a result, Traditionalists tend to be very respectful of seniority, title, and rank. Because the Great Depression and World War II shaped their world outlook, Traditionalists have a very practical view (make do, reuse, recycle) and know how to put money away for a rainy day. In addition, they grew up in a time when sacrifice for country was expected, so doing the right thing, no matter the cost to themselves, is how they live and work. They saw their fathers retire from the company at which they started, they saw few females in the workplace, and technology for most of their working life was not a factor. Reward and recognition are not important to them; remember, this is a generation that saved our country as we know it, and are just now having a memorial built to commemorate their valiant efforts. They grew up in a time when doing the right thing for your family, your company, and your country meant all three would do the "right" thing by you.

## KEY TRADITIONALIST VALUES: SELF-SACRIFICE, LOYALTY, AND DEDICATION

Baby Boomers

Born between 1946 and 1964, Baby Boomers invented the 60-hour workweek. They are competitive, to their own detriment at times, with a "work-till-you-drop" work ethic. Their parents (Traditionalists) raised them to be independent, to work hard, and not to complain. As there have been so many of them (hence Baby Boomers), they are used to competition and are competitive by nature, and love the thrill of competition, the thrill of victory. As they enter the ages when traditionally one would think about retirement, for the most part they have no plans for porches, rocking chairs, or seats at bingo tables. Retirement is not the end of a career, but the start of a career transition. They are optimistic about their own lives, believing that if they set goals and work hard, they can achieve whatever they set out to do. They also believe everyone should work hard to get where they want to go; if you don't make it, that is tough and your fault, and you must accept the consequences. Boomers have less respect for rank and hierarchy than their Traditionalist parents, but they still respect the hierarchy of leadership, especially when they can be part of it. They set long-term goals and have the "no pain-no gain" attitude to see them through. This generation believes hard work is the key to success, and if you put enough muscle into it, the world is your oyster.

Key Boomer Values: Working hard, playing hard, and competing to win

## GENERATION X

Born between 1965 and 1979, Gen X's are the free agents of the workforce, independent, self-reliant, and entrepreneurial. Because they don't find any value in wasting time with non-essential stuff, they shattered the management philosophy of "if ain't broke, don't fix it." With two career parents, Gen X's grew up alone and became the first latch key kids. In addition, 40% of their parents were divorced and/or lost their jobs during the '80s and '90s, and having witnessed that, Gen X does not see the payoff in career and company loyalty. As a result, Gen X's are very concerned about life balance and fiercely protective of family time. In addition, their parents, most likely overcompensating for divorcing and working too hard, spoiled this generation and did not want to see their kids have to work as hard as "they" did. As a result, Gen X's (like Millennials) have relied on help and support from their parents, giving them more flexibility in terms of sacrifice for career success. Gen X's tend to be skeptical and pragmatic, and value leadership by competence, not by position. They have little respect for service, title, or rank, because their parents had all three and lost their jobs anyway. Their career paths create a mosaic of work, learning, family, and even sabbatical. When they see their Boomer boss' being the last to leave every night they do not think, "Wow, she works hard" but instead, "Wow, she must have no life." Often experts label this generation as a little angry, as they struggle to achieve, or even come close to the financial success their parents had. This generation wants the success of their parents without having to dedicate their lives to their careers.

## KEY GEN X VALUES: LIFE BALANCE AND RESPECT FOR INDIVIDUALITY

Generation Y (also known as Millennials)

Born between 190 and 2000, Gen Y's are a generation that is divided; some are very hard workers and entrepreneurial, while others are less motivated and driven. Those who worked at legitimate jobs before they left high school see the payoff of working hard. Gen Y's grew up in a world of technology, with instant gratification and answers and reward at their fingertips. They've never known a world without mobile devices and 24/7 connectivity. They see themselves as citizens of the world and feel very connected through the Internet. Gen Y's fly to Europe to visit friends and family as easily as Traditionalists and Boomers crossed state lines. Spring break for them was Mexico or Costa Rica, not their parents' trip to Myrtle Beach, South Carolina. They have better relationships with their parents than many Gen X's and Boomers; their parents actively engaged them in decision-making and took interest in their thoughts and ideas. As a benefit of that, they have a strong interest in teamwork, but from day one they expect the CEO to seek out their opinion. Millennials have now surpassed Boomers as the largest generation. They are interested in career and leadership, but unlike the Traditionalists and Boomers, this is a generation that grew up getting a trophy for everything and having their parents attend every sporting event and school activity. This generation is open to and very much needs mentoring.

Gen Y Values: Making a difference in the world and instant gratification

## CONSIDERING GENERATIONAL ISSUES – WHY THIS MATTERS

In other words, our workplace is changing. Conventional wisdom would say that the Traditionalists and Baby Boomers are aging out, approaching retirement, and that because of that they may be resistant to the kinds of changes that need to be made.

Gallup's State of the American Workplace Report explains this nicely:

The U.S. workplace is in the midst of a generational shift with Traditionalists disappearing, Baby Boomers approaching their retirement years, and Millennials are entering the workforce in increasing numbers. Yet as the ranks of the youngest generation swell in the workplace, so too does their discontent. .

No wonder we are struggling with employee engagement: We have different attitudes, different ideas, and different perspectives on what work is, as well as how we should show up, how long we should work, and how we should behave in the work environment.Traditionalists and Baby Boomers may be headed towards retirement, but that does not necessarily mean they are retiring; many are holding onto their leadership positions, or at least holding onto the purse strings and control.

That represents a serious hurdle: Millennials and their needs are influencing the workplace, but the older generations and their models of business and engagement still hold the power. The Traditionalists and Boomers, while still struggling with engagement themselves, are more likely to conform to rules or leadership's direction. Meanwhile the Gen X's and Millennials, still struggling to find meaning in their work, can come off as resistant to older leadership models.

So what does all this mean for you as a leader? It means you have to work harder at communicating, understanding, and building respect across generations. It means, again, that engaging employees is not a one-size-fits-all program, and you are going to have to create a more inclusive and flexible workplace culture. However, in the end, it will be up to the employee, no matter his generation or his level in the organization, to decide whether or not to engage.

As a key part of the paradigm shift, everyone needs to realize that they are all responsible for owning their part in engagement. While leaders need to create inviting cultures, it is in the end up to the individual to engage.

## STATISTICS HOLD THE KEY

If you want to build a successful employee engagement program, then begin with the research, statistics hold the key. Doing your homework on the front end; understanding how the generations are different and how they are the same; and knowing what you are looking for in an employee and who you want to engage will ensure you have what you need to build a solid program.

Before you invest in creating a program, hiring experts, or developing a task force, take the time, as a leadership team, to read about the issue of engagement. Study it and, most importantly, discuss it. Be able, as a group, to answer and agree about how you see the generations are different, how they are the same, and what you are looking for in an employee. Taking the time to do that will ensure you build a program that matches your needs as well as those of the employee you bring on as a new team member.

Gallup (www.gallup.com) offers some solid generational insights. Their in-depth research solves the mysteries around just what it is that the majority of any specific workforce segment wants most, and underlines the fact that at the heart of it we are all human beings, emotional creatures, who at the core want and prioritize the same things.

At the end of the day, people are not all that different, however there are things that impact and influence us based on when we were born and how we grew up. So, understanding, in general, what drives a specific group's engagement and how that might help you to motivate individuals on your team can be a powerful tool. Keep in mind that these facts, as they relate to the generations, are highly generalized.

While Millennials, Generation X's, and Baby Boomers, all look for an opportunity to use their skills and do their best, along with a strong purpose that keeps them onboard and engaged, how they go about finding it is slightly different.

Learning more about the generations is great "background" information to have as your leaders go about creating your employee engagement program.

Now, while each generation may have a different perspective and take on life, depending on when they entered the workforce, at the end of the day, what they want from an employer and a job still comes back to being a part of something bigger, doing work that matters, and having a leader who cares.

## THE REAL WORD:

*David Long is the author of the Wall-Street-Journal-Bestselling book Built To Lead – 7 Management R.E.W.A.R.D.S. Principles for Becoming a Top 10% Manager and the CEO of MyEmployees.com,* a twenty-six-year-old firm in the top 1% worldwide in the employee engagement and recognition industry. David is a leader who leads on his own terms, and much of his success is rooted in his unorthodox but wise views on building teams and engaging employees.

David has always believed that this idea of treating employees differently based on their generations is not only the latest fad, but also a waste of time, energy, and, most importantly, resources. His belief, and much of his success, is his practice of treating all of his employees the same. He treats them all with  respect and dignity, and how he as a leader wants to be treated.

His team of 54 highly talented and fully engaged employees is a mix of generations, backgrounds, and skills. Instead of trying to adjust his organization to better suit each generation, David hires based on a shared set of values, beliefs, and work ethic. When team members have those things in common, it does not matter what generation they are from, only that you as an employer invest in their dreams, make them a part of yours, and ensure they understand and believe their work matters.

It is hard to believe, but the Bureau of Labor Statistics says that today's typical worker stays at his or her job for only about 4.4 years. And while that does not sound too appealing or long to the average employer, that number is actually expected to trend down now, as Millennials begin to outnumber Boomers in the workforce. Millennials' responses to this survey and their overall feelings on workplace longevity are closer to 2 to 2.5 years.

As a leader today, you need to understand that today's employees, those you are trying to recruit, develop, and retain, have a very different understanding of today's workplace. They did not grow up in a world of workplace stability, pensions, or job longevity. Their economy is global, and distrust of authority (governments and corporations) is a social norm. This all has greatly shaped how they *view and experience today's workplace. It has impacted the things they want from you as a leader and an employer. So you need to begin there. Rather than blaming your employees for not engaging, begin by understanding how society has changed and understanding this new type of employee, who they are, what they want, and how, together, you can ensure they get it.*

## CALL TO ACTION

1. *Understand Today's Employees Are Different – Begin here, and forget as a leader how you came up through the ranks, how you did what you "had" to do. Instead, start by understanding society as it is today, how that impacts today's employees and their journey, and how and why it needs to be very different from yours.*

2. *Brainstorm & Discover – Take a pause, a time out, and think about what you are looking for in an employee (what you value), and why some on your current team are engaged, why some are not. Talk with other leaders inside and outside your industry about what an engaged employee looks like, and how you know when someone is or is not engaged. Take the time to learn, discuss, and document what you are looking for, and what you are currently doing right to engage employees. Then review your process (or lack thereof) for how you reinforce those behaviors. Investing the time to do this will do wonders to ensure you create an employee engagement program that is right for you and for your company.*

3. *Take The Time – Take time to get to know your employees, who they are, what is important to them, and what*

*they value about your company. Learn their level of engagement, and what you can do to retain them, or get them even more engaged. Communication is a powerful, important tool, and you want to use it often to learn more about how to actively engage your employees. Taking this step will begin to position you as someone willing to invest in your employees before you ask them to invest in you.*

# CHAPTER 3

## THE SORRY STATE OF EMPLOYEE ENGAGEMENT

Honestly, I would describe the current state of employee engagement at not only an all-time low, but really kind of sad. That is basically all you need to know. Just kidding! But things are not good, meaning even more of your employees or team members than you realize may be checked out or job hunting (while still pretending to be present at work) instead of being fully focused and giving their all. Let's take a look at the cold, hard facts of the state of employee engagement.

Now, at the beginning of this book I shared some pretty sobering statistics: 70% of employees are currently disengaged; $450 billion is the current cost those disengaged workers are imposing on U.S. companies; and $700 million is currently being spent trying to solve the problem. And while those numbers are strong in and of themselves, recently I read an article in the Huffington Post (http://www.huffingtonpost.com/jeff-fermin/13-disturbing-facts-about_b_6140996.html) by Jeff Fermin, where he cited some additional disturbing facts about the current state of employee engagement:

1. 88% of employees report not having or feeling any passion for their work

2. 80% of senior managers (those holding high level positions) re-

port being disengaged

3.  86% of HR managers and leaders report not having a good plan for leadership development

4.  70% of those HR leaders believe they have a significant retention and engagement problem

5.  75% of those HR leaders report they are struggling to attract and recruit top talent

6.  6% believe their current process for managing and rewarding performance is worth the time

7.  ⅔ of today's employees report feeling stressed out and overwhelmed

As we discussed before, we have a problem: We are spending more to solve the problem, yet the problem, despite our efforts, is getting worse.

## THE REAL WORLD

*Seems every leader has a story about an employee who is not engaged, or is frustrated by the growing number that seems to be out there. We hear terms like "entitled," "lacking work ethic," and "lazy" used to describe today's employees, but truthfully, you need to look deeper to understand what is going on.*

*In 2011, Joey Havens, then a partner of HORNE LLP, a Top-50 CPA Firm, was invited to put his name in the ring for HORNE's next executive partner. As part of this process, the firm asked Joey to present his vision for the firm's future in a town hall meeting with all of the partners. Realizing that the current state of engagement at HORNE wasn't enough to push the firm forward, Joey shared a vision of taking a journey together—of partners and team members engaging—to go from being a good firm to becoming a great firm. In order to be great, he shared a vision of building the Wise Firm, a term now used to describe their culture. The vision is based on the Biblical parable of the wise man and the foolish man. The wise man built his house on the rock, while the foolish man built his house on the sand. The storms came, the wind blew, and the water flowed and washed the foolish man's house away, but the wise man's house stood strong on a solid foundation. Much like the Wise Man, the Wise Firm is built on the solid foundation of "we" and "service," with all the blocks of the Wise Firm building toward empowered people who get results and share lots of positive energy.*

*Why the Wise Firm culture? Joey and his leadership team recognized that when people have a purpose and a clearly articulated vision, they will commit and engage to do great things together. A culture full of positive energy attracts great clients and great people. HORNE recognized that you must show you care first before your people will care.*

*Understanding that this idea of employee engagement is a two-way street, companies and leaders must intentionally build the right cultures to attract the right people, and employees need to choose to engage; this is what separates HORNE from others in their profession. In addition, this is the major message of this book: Everyone on the team, at every level, needs to own it, needs to take responsibility, and needs to invest and commit to making it work.*

## IN THEIR OWN WORDS...

Consider this from Forbes writer Josh Bersin: "Our research shows that we may need to change the way we manage people (end appraisals?), change the work environment (open offices? nap rooms? ping pong tables?), and change who we hire (are we hiring the right people for our mission, culture and values? are we assessing well?). All these things tend to go well beyond the typical engagement survey.

## THE IDEA

So while the research clearly demonstrates that employee engagement is in pretty bad shape, it is important to better understand what we mean when we say our employees are disengaged. In Gallup's The State of the American Workplace report, leading employee engagement experts define engaged workers into three categories:

Engaged – These employees feel profound passion for their work, and a deep connection to their organization and their mission. They are driven and innovative, and they move the organization forward by bringing in new ideas and the majority of new customers.

Not Engaged – These employees are actively checked out; they are showing up at work but just going through the motions, not putting passion, energy, or new ideas into their work.

Actively Disengaged – These employees have quit, or have stayed and are now on a mission to infect your other workers. They are actively working out their unhappiness and bringing down your engaged workers in the process.

While it is clear we all want our employees to fall into the category of "engaged," unfortunately, for most of us, fewer than one in three of our employees meet the requirements for that level; and as this trend continues, that number will soon fall to one in five. Yes, meaning that majority the people you employ will be at the least actively checked out, and at the worst, actively trying to negatively influence your culture.

So while it is clear that employees are disengaged, it is even more interesting and important to know the facts around what this is costing you as a leader and a company, and why you should care. And believe me, you should care! Now, stick with me, as I am about to get a little nerdy on you and dig deep into numbers and statistics. While not the most fun reading, pay attention, because this is interesting and definitely worth knowing. According again to this study done by Gallup, employee engagement plays a key role and is a strong indicator in the success of your company on several levels.

Gallup researched approximately 50,000 businesses and organizations that included over one million employees in 34 countries and discovered those that score in the top half of companies, with the highest levels of employee engagement, are more than twice as likely to be successful than those in the bottom half. In addition, those companies that truly prioritized employee engagement and finished in the 99th percentile have four times the success rate of other companies. Yes, four times the success rate.

Gallup, in their research, identified nine key performance indicators that are impacted by a high level of employee engagement vs. a company with below average employee engagement figures. Those with an above average of engagement employees experiences the following results:

* 37% lower absenteeism
* 25% lower turnover (in high-turnover organizations)
* 65% lower turnover (in low-turnover organizations)
* 28% less shrinkage
* 48% fewer safety incidents
* 41% fewer patient safety incidents
* 41% fewer quality incidents (defects)
* 10% higher customer metrics

* 21% higher productivity

* 22% higher profitability

These statistics demonstrate the level at which your employees are engaged, and how much they care about your company, are passionate about their jobs, and are focused on the experience. This directly transfers to your productivity, your customer experience, and your ability to attract more top talent and to add to your bottom line. In fact, I believe in this economy, it is the only thing truly differentiating you from your competition; with so many costs either fixed or rising, more deeply engaging your employees is your only real chance of growing your organization and increasing your bottom line results.

Unfortunately, as we have shared, the state of employee engagement is not only bad, but actually getting worse. Even with our efforts as leaders and our focus on the problem, the numbers of disengaged employees just continue to rise. Within the next few years, if something does not change, employee disengagement is expected to rise from 70 to 84%, and that rise will cause the costs to companies to rise from $450 billion to more than $550 billion, forcing us to spend even more (upwards of $1.5 billion) trying to get our employees to engage.

So we can agree it is bad and getting worse. The real tragedy, however, is that we are continuing to use the same old tactics and strategies to solve what has become a new type of problem. The research shows that what we are doing clearly is not working, so let's get off this merry-go-round by first learning how we got on it.

## CALL TO ACTION

1. *Impact – Take note of the impact of the lack of engagement—the havoc it is causing in areas such as absenteeism, decreased productivity, and turnover.*

2. *Measure – If you are not measuring some of the things mentioned in this chapter, then start. The better you understand where lack of engagement impacts you, the better you will be able to target your approach to ensuring that an increase in engagement creates and increase in results.*

3. *Imagine – Picture what even a 10% increase in employee engagement could do for your company, your customers, and your shareholders.*

# CHAPTER 4

## OUR TRADITIONAL APPROACH

n my book Winning in the Trust & Value Economy, I make the case that a business hoping to succeed is one that makes "change" an integral part of its overall business strategy. One of the major indicators of success of those companies I interviewed for the book was their ability to be nimble and flexible to take advantage of opportunity and minimize threat. In today's economy, "change" is a business strategy.

Now, given that employees are your greatest competitive advantage, I am going to add that redefining approaches to employee engagement must take a leading role in business strategy as well. In the past, the job of engaging employees often fell to Human Resource leaders and department managers; in today's economy, employee engagement needs to be elevated to the executive level and become an integral part of the overall business strategy.

Deloitte (a highly respected financial advisory firm) produced a report in 2015, "Global Human Capital Trends," in which they point out that nearly 80% of world business leaders see engagement and employee retention as "urgent matters." They might as easily, and accurately, describe them as competitive differentiators in the modern business world, too.

To grow and remain competitive, any business requires employees who are passionate about their work, connected and committed to their company/employer, and on the same proverbial page as leadership. To succeed in today's Trust & Value Economy, a modern business needs more than buyers and a good business strategy; it requires a team that proactively exceeds demands. To have that means attracting, retaining, and then fully engaging top talent. In today's business environment, the quality of your employees and team is your only competitive advantage.

Unfortunately, as we have already learned, employee engagement is at an all-time low, costing billions and yet remaining an ongoing and growing concern. Companies are keenly aware of the problems and challenges brought about by the lack of employee engagement. The Deloitte data further revealed that approximately 25% of the workforce will seek to change jobs in 2015, and that the majority of this job changing group will be the most skilled or motivated. That means that what few engaged employees you have, if you do not adjust your engagement strategy, you will most likely lose, and most likely lose to your competition.

Suffering the loss of engaged employees will do far more than alter the environment in the workplace, it will prevent you as a leader and a company from maintaining the stability and energy you need to thrive in the modern, global market. A loss of engaged workers will actually blunt your ability to respond to the "pull" economy in which, as you remember from Winning in the Trust & Value Economy, the customer makes the rules.

A "rude awakening" may just be the opportunity we need to learn valuable lessons. Clearly, for almost all companies there is room for improvement in the employee engagement process, and no one is free from putting employee engagement at the top of their "to do" list. So where do we start? By really digging into the current state of employee engagement. We have scratched the surface, but we need to understand why this is happening and what specifically is going wrong.

## THE PROBLEMS

We have the facts and figures, and we see the financial impact of disengaged workers. Low productivity results in hundreds of billions lost to U.S. businesses. Understand, this is not just a U.S. problem; the issue of employee disengagement is felt worldwide. A study in the U.K. determined that roughly ⅔ of their workforce is actively disengaged, meaning hundreds of billions more in losses there as well. These same figures appear in all parts of the globe. While not good news, it is somewhat comforting to know we are not alone!

So, where is it all going wrong? What is so bad about traditional employee engagement practices that allow them to fail on such a massive scale? There are a few answers to those questions.

## MISSING THE OBVIOUS

You have to begin with leadership perspective. While most leaders recognize there is a problem, most fail to realize that the current strategies are out of date, given the new economy and the changing employee. Failing to recognize and constantly assess what is and what is not working about your current employee engagement program leaves any business vulnerable to the loss of top employees.

We are now living in a highly competitive market, a global economy, one where competition is fierce and consumers are in control. Expecting the strategies and tactics we used ten to fifteen years ago to still work in today's environment is like using a fax machine when everyone you communicate with has upgraded to a scanner.

Think about it: We are spending more than $700 million on employee engagement and retention, yet you still easily lose your best workers to aggressive firms, or to those who are a few steps ahead in the employee engagement game. If we are spending that type of money and not seeing improvement, why do we keep doing the same thing over and over and expecting a different result? I believe that Albert Einstein said that is the very definition of insanity. Well, when it comes to today's approach to employee engagement, the statistics and the amount of money we are spending tell us it is clearly time for a new approach.

Just as a business owner must accept that her customers have the entire global marketplace from which to choose, she also must realize that the job market is wide open to employees as well. Statistics reveal that about ¼ of the workforce is switching jobs in 2015, making it clear that employees (the good ones) are as aware of the vast opportunities for employment as your customers are aware of your competition. Again, we live in an economy where getting customers or employees is not really that hard, but getting good ones can be a serious challenge.

In other words, do not assume you can treat employees "any old way." Yes, there are problems in the job markets, and openings may seem limited, but those statistics reveal one huge truth: The most skilled and high-performing workers are the ones slated to look for employment elsewhere, and they will be the ones who will easily find it.

Think of it like sales. Finding a customer is not a problem, but finding one whom you like, who pays your price easily, and who loves to buy your products and services is much harder to find. The same goes for employees. You may find people to work, but getting the ones that fully engage takes another level of strategy.

Additionally, the Internet has made it amazingly easy for those employees at the top of their games to learn about, seek out, and obtain jobs quickly and competitively, and other companies are eagerly using the Internet to seek out your top performers. Trust me; if you are not actively engaging your workers, someone else is.

All too often, employee engagement strategies and programs are created, left in strategy form, and stored on a shelf of the Human Resources Department; or worse they are privy to a big kick-off event and announcement, but without any action taking place.

## THE REAL WORLD

*Lloyd Cartwright, now president and CEO of a very successful community bank, had once been a promising young leader with a large financial institution, a company that had invested more than ten years in his education and career development with the intent that he rise through the ranks and be among the top leaders of the company.*

*In preparation, Lloyd, along with twelve of his fellow associates, had been chosen to take part in a Leadership Program designed by a high-powered external consultant specifically for the development of the firm's talent. As part of this program, these twelve future leaders would work on a project designed to solve one of the firm's major challenges. Preselected by current leadership, these challenges represented some of the biggest issues facing the company, and these next level leaders were called to work together to tackle the issues, present solutions to the current leadership, and with their approval, go about implementing them.*

*The concept was beautiful: have the firm's current leadership define some of the major opportunities and challenges facing the organization, then have the "high potentials" work to come up with innovative and creative ideas and implement their plans. In conception, the plan worked perfectly; leadership did their part, even setting aside an entire day to listen to future leaders present their programs.*

*And present these high potential leaders did, after working an entire year on their projects. Their presentations were well thought-out, well researched, and well delivered, and met with rave reviews from leadership. Leadership left the session vowing to give final approval to the plans within the week, fund the initiatives, and give the high potentials the go-ahead to begin implementation. That is where everything fell apart. While their intentions were good, leadership never met, never gave any more thought or consideration to the ideas and plans their high potentials had created, let alone funding those projects. Within two years, ten of the original twelve, including Lloyd, had left the company.*

*That is one of the major problems with traditional programs; that is all they are, just programs. All too often, they are separate initiatives, outside of the corporate strategy, and something into which leadership puts lots of words and resources, but very little action.*

## FLAWED TRADITIONS

I would say that a primary problem with traditional leadership programs is that they are well traditional. Traditions are great, but there are times, like this when the economy has shifted, when we really need to back up and ask ourselves if we are using traditional programs because they work or because they are traditions.

Now we have only to look at the statistics to understand that is certainly true of traditional strategies for employee engagement. It is hard to believe, but some of the strategies we use today to engage our employees actually date back to the late 19th century. Many are habitual, standard procedures, simply going through the motions, and doing what we have always done expecting a different result.

Many of the employee engagement practices we use today date back to not only a different time, but a different economy. Though Gallup and other firms created the whole notion of engagement surveys, and pioneered the idea of employee engagement as a result (sometime in the 1990s), their origins date back much farther than that. It actually dates back to the American steel industry in the late 1800s, when industrial engineer Frederick Taylor explored the effect of attitude on performance among steel workers of the era.

Now, think about a steel plant in the late 1800's, hardly the same working environments or employees that we encounter today, yet most of the traditional strategies at work in employee engagement begin and end with those classic surveys. For the most part, we are still using the same methods and ideas we used in that economy, in those times, and expecting them to work now. If we have accepted that the world of business has changed, and that the way that we do business has to change, then it is simple logic to recognize that the way we approach employee engagement definitely has to change too.

Of course, it is not as easy as making up your mind and doing it. The way we go about engaging employees, the systems and processes we create, have been building up over the course of decades in our companies, and current leadership may be so heavily invested in them that necessary changes are a little too far out of their comfort zone.

I found this so interesting when I wrote Winning in the Trust & Value Economy, as professionals, we become so invested in what we are doing that, even if it is not working, even if the statistics and results prove it, we still struggle to change.

Understanding that it is important that we start small. I love the idea of employee engagement surveys, but maybe it is time for a new approach to how we and our employees engage in using them. Rather than sending out your typical employee engagement surveys according to an annual Human Resources calendar, then simply filing away the reports, and ticking them off the "to do" list, it is vital that, as a leader, you step outside of your comfort zone and routine. Take the surveys off automation; reassess, reinvigorate, and really scrutinize them. In addition, understand that a survey is worthless if trust is not built into the culture first, and if leadership does not hold themselves accountable to take action.

If there ever was a time when "out with the old and in with the new" fit, it is now, and that motto needs to be your key business strategy. Now, do not worry; this doesn't mean that surveys will become a thing of the past, but it does mean that they cannot become fixed, routine, or copied from a basic template. If you are going to continue to use employee engagement surveys (and it is fine if you do, fine if you do not), then you need to create a survey employees want to fill out, and one they trust you will use. Your survey needs to be something that gives you information and feedback that will really help you enhance and reinvigorate your employee engagement program.

## THE TRUST FOUNDATION

As we mentioned before, trust is the very foundation of any employee engagement survey, and your employees need to believe that you are open to their feedback and are willing to use their suggestions and ideas. Humanizing employee engagement surveys, making them more along the lines of coaching and customer feedback, is a great first step, but the true power of the survey is in the belief your team has that you want the feedback. In addition, they need to trust that you will take the time to share and communicate the information you received from them, and that you have a plan of action that you will implement. To engage employees, you need more than generic, automated methods or outdated approaches; you need commitment to the process and to change.

## THE "UNENGAGEMENT" SURVEY

Think about the word "generic" for a moment. It is a no-name brand: blank, bland, undefined. It is also how I would describe many of the current or traditional employee engagement surveys, programs, and resources available and used today. You can just as easily use more colorful terms such as "one size fits all", "umbrella", or "plain vanilla" when explaining the design of traditional employee engagement strategies.

The meanings add up to the same thing, and that is there is a tremendous problem. By depersonalizing employee engagement surveys, by using a generic approach, we not only lack feedback from our employees, but we send a strong message that we do not really care. It is like buying someone a birthday card that simply says happy birthday, versus making them one, or buying one with a message that is personalized to them. By taking the time to custom design a survey, you are showing the employees you are interested, you care, and that you understand what is important to them.

In addition, asking for general, non-specific information will result in general, non-specific answers. Worse yet, how your employee engagement survey is designed and what feedback you ask for sends a strong message to your team about how serious you are about wanting to know what they think, feel, and need. Use a generic survey, and you will send the wrong message loud and clear.

## THE REAL WORLD

*A few years ago, I was working with Bob, a CEO who was at the time transitioning into his role after being a senior level leader with his organization for more than ten years. A bright, young, innovative leader, Bob knew his company (which was doing well) was capable of more, and he wanted to be the leader who made it happen. Bob was a visionary who understood that to make it happen, he was going to need to fully engage his team, and that a survey was a great place to start.*

*Together we customized the survey, got lots of input, and created thought-provoking questions. We made the decision that, in addition to taking the survey company-wide, I would do some one-on-one feedback sessions to really go deep on some issues. I was all set to go, Bob felt good about the process, and, for my part, I thought, "Yes, finally a leader who gets it, someone who understands that in order to engage employees, you have to be willing to go out on a limb and get real, solid employee feedback."*

*That is when the phone call came. Bob called me in a panic; he had just learned that a deal to sell part of the company (a deal that had been in the works for a while and had not been public knowledge) had finally come through, and he was going to make the announcement by the end of the month. Bob had called because, while this was a very good thing for the company, he was worried about the employees, and how they might react as news of change on any level always ensures a reaction of fear. Because of that, Bob wanted me to hurry up and send out the surveys and complete the more "focused" sessions so the feedback would not be impacted by this news.*

That is how rooted we are in "traditional employee surveys"—even an innovative, young leader like Bob, who understands he needs his team to fully engage to move forward, does not understand that the point of a survey is to really understand what your employees are thinking, feeling, and needing. Given that, there was never a better time to do a survey than after Bob made the announcement.

Feedback is valuable only when it is real, and no employee who is fully engaged, in my humble opinion, can answer a survey honestly without providing ideas for changes, solutions, or places for improvement. If you are not getting challenging, innovative or negative feedback when doing a survey, it is time for a redesign.

## THE VALUE OF EMPLOYEE FEEDBACK

There are three very important reasons to gain "non-traditional" employee feedback, three benefits to you as both the employer and the employee:

1. You send a strong message that you care, that you are interested, and that what your employees say and think matters.

2. You get valuable information, a baseline as to what is most important to your team.

3. You get buy-in and ownership; when employees express their opinions, they take the first step to having skin in the game.

To succeed in today's global economy, we need to differentiate ourselves and create a niche. The same thing applies to our employees: We have to differentiate our culture, create something special, if we want to attract "special" employees. Traditional engagement methods use a general approach meant to generally appeal to a general employee population, one that is hardly targeted at meeting the needs of the best and brightest employees.

## POORLY DEFINING EMPLOYEE ENGAGEMENT

The Delloite surveys proved that a huge number of companies surveyed felt that their employee engagement processes were "weak" (more than 55%), and only 6% felt that their processes for employee engagement were worth the time and costs. Yet, even knowing this, they still go through the motions, collecting that data and attempting to work with it. Think about that: Only 6% believe their data has any value, yet they do it anyway. The result? A disaster, as a bad or generic survey is worse than none at all, costing the companies large sums of money and resources but yielding ever-increasing rates of disengagement.

General questions and generic surveys are, in my opinion, indicative of a wider problem: Companies may not even have a firm definition of employee engagement, or grasp why they need it.

In fact, one report noted that "a quick search for definitions... yielded results as varied as simple happiness, satisfaction with an employer, pride in one's work, willingness to drive business success, and commitment to act in the employer's best interests" (Association for Talent Development, 2015). Almost a decade ago, Gallup offered a basic definition of employee engagement: "working with passion... [and] finding a profound emotional connection to one's company."

So think about that, and begin by asking yourself, "What is my definition of employee engagement?" and, "Where can solid engagement take my firm, as well as the employees themselves?" Gaining clarity and leadership consensus on this is a critical step in developing a powerful employee engagement program; if you have no idea what you want from employees, how can you use what you learn from them about satisfaction, dissatisfaction, influence, and so on? Once you gain clarity on why you want your employees to engage, you open yourself up to creating "real" surveys and using the data to truly improve your company.

## FLAWED INTERPRETATIONS

I love this new economy, because so much that we held dear, believed in, and lived by has been turned upside down. The old adage that people leave "managers and not organizations" is actually not exactly true in today's Trust & Value economy. The statistics, reports, and studies all point to a more complex issue: A combination of things can make people leave their jobs. We lose our valuable employees not over one thing or one person these days, but often by a surprising blend of organizational issues, such as lack of leadership, accountability, or clear direction, all which cause or contribute to low employee retention or high turnover.

To prevent this from happening, and to get off the traditional treadmill, you need to shake up your approach to communicating with, taking an interest in, and getting feedback from your employees. A few of my preferred methods will help you prevent getting the same old answers, having bias in your interpretation of their answers, or just going through the motions and not getting anything of value.

1. Focus Groups or Individual Interviews – Randomly choose 5-10% of your workforce to participate in some focus groups or individual interviews. Getting them involved in a deeper discussion will give you a better understanding of what your employees are saying. Your focus here needs to be on open-ended questions and listening.

2. Outside Consultant – Use someone with no preconceived ideas of or history with your company to perform the survey and determine the outcomes. Use this individual for both your survey and interviews, then have that person compile the data and identify themes.

3. Employee Interpretation – Ask again, a random group of employees to interpret the results. While, yes, this will still leave you open to bias, it is better to have their bias than yours as a leader.

## PASSING THE BUCK AND MISSING THE MARK

If you really want to shatter the traditional approach to employee engagement (and you should, because, again, traditional is not working), you need to get it off the Human Resources desk and onto the desk of the CEO.

## THE REAL WORLD

*When Joey Havens assumed the role of executive partner with HORNE LLP, he made the vision of building the Wise Firm culture with his team members the firm's top priority. This journey required sharing the vision over and over with all of the firm's 500 team members. He prioritized spending time with team members to hear their ideas, concerns, and needs. While he worked closely with partners, Human Resources, the communication director, and even outside consultants, at the end of the day, the jobs of people recruitment, retention, development, and engagement started with him, and the buck stopped with him.*

*HORNE's partners and team members have embraced the vision, and Joey is focused on serving his team (developing, communicating with, retaining, and learning with and from them). At HORNE, success is measured by creating positive energy, realizing full potential for team members and clients, and having team members engage and lead in their journey to become the Wise Firm.*

## SKIN IN THE GAME

While I believe that hiring professionals, tapping into external resources, and working closely with Human Resources and Learning & Development can be tremendous assets when building an engagement program, at the end of the day, if the CEO does not play a key role, he sends a loud message that employee engagement is not his core focus. Lack of CEO level involvement on the issue of employee engagement is yet another example of a traditional method that is so outdated it is nearly pointless.

In addition, the employees need to be the other key player. Traditional programs and methods of employee engagement provide the system through which the employee is to engage. Again, it is an outdated method, because the very definition of engagement is feeling included and connected. If you leave out the employee in the development of the process, then you lose a key opportunity to get their buy-in, interest, or support. And without that, they never really engage.

Why? Because traditional methods put the responsibility of engagement on the Human Resources department, not where it belongs, between both the employer (CEO) and the employee. This flawed focus has to be turned around if you truly want to build and implement an impactful employee engagement program. It is not all about workers, nor is it entirely up to management to keep everyone happy; it is all about the collaboration between leadership and employees. People support what they help create, and for true engagement to happen, everyone needs skin in the game.

## GETTING YOUR FOCUS RIGHT

It has to start at the top, and that means including the leadership team, middle management, frontline managers, and so on. Unless the executives want to nurture true engagement and practice it themselves, it is never going to happen. I want to repeat this it is so important, this is the difference between going through the motions and really creating a program that works.

### THE REAL WORLD

*Rebecca, a top female executive with a large financial firm, was sharing her thoughts on the state of employee engagement at a panel discussion at a conference in New York City. When asked what the biggest stumbling block was to creating attracting, retaining, and developing top talent, her response was "current leadership." Her point was that until leadership embraces engagement as THEIR job, until they are held accountable for the development of people, and until they embrace the fact that today's employees learn and work differently, nothing is going to change.*

*It is for this reason that the modern business model, the current way we go about engaging employees, has to be turned on its head. Success requires the focus of employee engagement to be fine-tuned and yet all-inclusive, requiring that all involved become a constant part of the process in a way that is more hands-on and engaged than ever.*

*Engagement has to actually "engage" the individual, meaning they have to be part of the process, and it simultaneously has to be the responsibility of leadership. Thus, the focus is not entirely on the workforce or even on individuals alone; it is a shared responsibility. This creates the new business model of collaborative leadership.*

## TRADITION IS FAILING

Experts and academics have posited many reasons why employee engagement surveys and initiatives fail, and they include:

- That the firms might lack a culture that encourages employees to thrive.
- That leadership misinterprets data from surveys or fails to act on it.
- That leadership is hesitant to offer recognition.
- That companies do not offer career paths for those who perform well.
- That communication is poor.
- That expectations are not made clear.
- That a firm lacks the clearly stated values that motivate workers.
- That firms don't know what employees want.

Yes, those are large-scale problems, but they demonstrate the kind of invaluable data that employees are willing to provide if someone is listening and ready to act. Before even undertaking an employee engagement survey or program, you need to know if leadership is prepared to act on what your employee engagement surveys uncover.

As one journalist so eloquently explains: "Right now, scores of executives and their teams are spending countless hours plotting on how to best engage those who are closest to the customer. Yet few bother to ask these people for suggestions on what can be done to increase employee commitment and productivity" (Forbes, 2015).

That is a wonderful illustration of the new economic model—the customers rule, the workforce is the group closest to and most likely to engage with the customer, and leadership is responsible for ensuring this formula works favorably for all.

However, your next step is to recognize one key fact from all of this information, and it is this: that engagement is not just the responsibility of the employee or management, but of all involved.

An entirely new approach to leadership, team building, and teamwork is needed. You have a role as a leader, but your employees have a role in engagement too.

The old methods of employee engagement no longer work. In fact, statistics show that they hardly worked at all in the past. It is time to let them go and restructure your approach to this issue.

There are benefits for everyone when such changes are made, and your next steps include the creation of a collaborative approach to building a dedicated, inclusive, and even multi-generational team.

## CALL TO ACTION

Self-Assess - Begin by asking yourself if you too are guilty of remaining stuck in this older perspective.

**LEADERSHIP:**

Have you created a clear definition of employee engagement?

Have you included employee engagement in your overall business strategy?

Have (and how have you) embraced the fact that your workers are the key to your ability to compete in the global marketplace?

**EMPLOYEES:**

Are you waiting for someone else to engage you? Why?

What are you doing to ensure your next steps for skill enhancement or career development?

Have you embraced that this is your life, your career, so it is your responsibility to engage? If so, how?

Hundreds of millions of dollars are being thrown at fast solutions to an increasingly disengaged workforce, yet none of these approaches holds the answers.

So again, ask yourself:

Are you remaining too distant from the situation?

Are you hoping to pay someone else to motivate employees to be more engaged?

**DEFINE ROLES**

Emplyees and leaders need to work together to define roles, and create process' that are collaborative. Together you will build an organization that inspires ownership at every level!

# CHAPTER 5

## TIME TO TURN EMPLOYEE ENGAGEMENT ON ITS HEAD

"Times are a-changing," as Bob Dylan sang, and who knew he was talking about employee engagement! Okay, that is not true, but it could be.

While I wrote about this new economy and changing times in Winning in the Trust & Value Economy, so much that I shared is applicable to understanding how the state of employee engagement got in the shape it is in today. The underlying premise of the book is that in this new global economy, where competition is at an all-time high and consumers are in control, it is not what we sell but how we sell it that makes all the difference. It is all about building and developing trust with customers. To build trust with customers, you have to build trust with your employees.

This is an economy where we need good customers and good employees far more than they need us, and we cannot take that or them for granted. There is a whole world of opportunities open to them (customers and employees) with a few clicks of a mouse or swipes on a mobile device screen. That change means we need a radically different model for business, a model that takes it from a market in which predicting fluctuations or creating a new system takes a back seat to understanding the customer and meeting his needs. This shift is also permanent, as we know, because business is never going back to the way that it was.

Why? Because a global, high-tech economy puts the consumer in control, and whether you are the shop on the corner or the multinational with branches on most continents, you must adhere to this new model, this new consumer, or be left in the dust.

Customer experience has become the new indicator of how well your business will perform and if it will grow. This is not a customer experience as we know it in the traditional sense, not just satisfaction; you have to ensure that you create a relationship with your customers that will override the conveniences or prices that others might offer. After all, a better deal or a more attractive website is a tap or click away, so it is imperative to keep your clients happy and motivated to buy from you.

Employees, the good and talented ones, are no different. A new job is almost as easy for your top performers to find, often just a click away or one connection via social networking. Just like you have to create relationships with your customers that motivate them to buy from you, you need to create a relationship with your employees that makes your company an "irresistible organization," one that attracts the best and the brightest employees.

Your organization must be able to pivot and change as needed, making it the ideal place to engage innovative and talented future leaders. In today's economy, getting employees to engage is about attracting them to your business and then getting them to want to commit and stay. Getting top performers to commit is the ultimate key to success in the modern economy.

## BUILDING YOUR ADVANTAGE

In the new economy, customer experience is the path to profitability, and to create that path for your customers you need to build an amazing experience for your employees.

Gone are the days when you could take your workforce for granted or treat employees like a cog in the machine of industry or commerce. In an economy where "what" we sell has become a commodity, but "how" we sell it is our competitive advantage, our employees have become our greatest strength, our only market differentiator, and the most important asset we have.

Again, for those of us who have been in the workforce for years, this is different from the traditional perspective. Before a global, high-tech economy, we had far more control over where customers shopped, or where people could work. Sure, customer experience was important, and the treatment of employees mattered, but if you screwed up, neither your customers nor your employees had much choice. Today, they do, so the only reason customers are buying from you, the only reasons employees are working with you, is the experience and culture you create. As one HR manager has said, "Employees don't want a career, they want an experience" (Forbes, 2014).

So, how do you give your employees the experiences they want and need in order to provide your customers with the type of positive experiences they deserve? This is easier said than done, as it is a complex issue. However, the return on investment makes it more than worth the effort.

## STEP OUTSIDE YOUR COMFORT ZONE...ASAP

A shift in the global economy should be enough to push you out of your comfort zone and get you out of your box, but when you also consider the startling statistics of the deteriorating state of engagement, you should be ready to go so far away that you cannot even see the box. So much has changed in today's business world that the door has opened to an absolute need for an innovative and very different approach to employee engagement. The leaders who embrace the idea that talented employees are your most important strategic assets, and who put employee engagement at the top of their priority list, will be the ones who will take the lead in this new economy.

Again, this is a complex problem that can't be solved with a singular, "one size fits all" approach; it demands a new style of leadership with a series of fresh behaviors, patterns, and tactics. Creating an employee experience is about using  a range of approaches, and having an openness to do things a different way. Right there we see a major shift, one I already mentioned. Rather than being a step along the annual Human Resource pathway, your employee engagement program must now become a working part of your business strategy. It is a process that will touch each employee as he or she is hired, on-boarded, and moved along the pathways in the organization.

It is a strategy that begins with a clearly defined identity, mission, and culture; in other words, a definition of the purpose of the company that an employee can then tie himself to. Though these terms are rarely something we see or include as part of a traditional engagement program, they are the new foundation, where the process all begins.

We see this every day in our culture, in an effort to attract customers and differentiate themselves in the market place, companies are rebranding themselves. For instance, we no longer hear about drug companies: We have come to call them health and wellness facilities. Local grocery stores have become organic markets, and gyms have become fitness studios.

Look at any major industry, from finance and banking to medicine and manufacturing, and you will see that those who have figured out how to hire and retain the best employees have made a point of clarifying what they are. They can easily communicate what they stand for, and how and why their employees matter. As author Joey Remain said in his book The Story of Purpose, people want to be part of something bigger than themselves.

If you take the time to first clarify your mission, culture and, identity your brand, your employees can then easily find a way to connect to it, and you will become the kind of irresistible organization where employees not only want to work, but want to fully engage.

## NOW IS THE TIME

I always seem to talk about the downside of change. Let me point out that change can be a good thing, a great thing, and that committing to it and to innovation can be incredibly rewarding.

The time to start is now. Rather than waiting until you lose another top associate or holding off until your usual annual survey and some sort of performance assessment, you need to begin changing now and engaging your employees now. Getting input, ideas, or feedback from your associates should not be an annual event but a consistent process that you begin today.

As a leader, you need to think about your employee as someone you listen to, rather than someone you tell to do something. Shift your paradigm to begin treating employees more like valued team members. Take the time to invest in learning who they are and what is important to them. As a leader, you can begin by listening to their ideas, and being authentic and real when asking for feedback and input.

## INDULGING IS NOT ENGAGING

The surveys and reports (including lists of the places ranked as the best to work due to employee satisfaction) tell us that it takes more than free lunches or nap rooms to engage an employee. It takes work. It takes things like good leadership, training and development, stimulation and attention to individual growth, clear definitions of purpose, inclusion, and provisions of work that matters.

Okay, there is a good chance you and your company are already using some of those less than successful approaches we looked at in the previous chapter. You might be using flat annual surveys, sticking to traditional methods of assessing performance, perhaps even using money as a motivator through annual appraisals and subsequent raises in earnings (or not). How are these methods working out? Consider that around eighty percent of companies perform some sort of engagement survey, and yet most admit they don't quite know how to interpret the results or how to improve on the scores. They even admit they have no idea if they are event working.

This tells us that most programs we are investing in, are doing nothing more than shooting in the dark, and we are just hoping to discover the "magic bullet" that turns things around. Well, unfortunately, hope and guessing are not the best strategies for successful change. To transform your organization it takes innovation, patience and focus. You cannot simply flick a switch and have a new, fully formed, and effective employee engagement program in place. If you could, I would not be writing books—I would be selling that program!

Let's begin by thinking about employee engagement and our employees from a different perspective. Let's begin  looking at your workforce as your customers, or, even more surprising, as your product. For a prime example, consider your approaches to customer service surveys, customer feedback, or even complaints. How are these handled, what attention do you give customer feedback, and how do you value customer input?

We have been conditioned to focus and react to customer feedback and complaints, and as leaders in the new economy, we need to take that hyper like focus and apply it to our employees. You would never let days or months go by without responding or acting on a customer complaint or idea, so you need to hold yourself to the same standards when it comes to your employees.

## TAKE OWNERSHIP TODAY

Employee engagement is a matter of ownership—at every level: employee, middle management, and CEO. Turning employee engagement upside down means taking much of the onus and focus off the employee's performance and turning the spotlight on collaborative effort and dedication to two-way communication.

It really is the responsibility of leadership to provide an environment where employees want to engage, but as we have been learning, that is not a culture that can be dictated; it is one that needs to include both

## IN THEIR OWN WORDS...

When writing about a new approach to employee engagement, one journalist had this to say: "Companies that understand this topic go beyond engagement surveys: they re-design jobs, they change the work environment, they add new benefits, they continuously develop managers, and they invest in people. They are 'mission-driven' and they make sure people are screened for culture and job fit (the wrong person cannot be 'engaged' regardless of what HR does)."

employees and leadership actively working together to create it.

Taking the responsibility is leadership's first step, and that means taking action as well. In this chapter, we have accepted that the new economy has created the need for an entirely different approach to employee management. We learned that the old ways of doing things are, well, "old," and that we have to literally turn things on their head, creating a dual responsibility between workers and leadership. If modern workers are eager to have an experience beyond just a job or even a career, they can only receive these things when their organizations have clearly defined missions, identities, and goals. In other words, it can only happen when leadership has first created the culture to allow or invite employees to engage.

---

## IN THEIR OWN WORDS...

"Gallup researchers studied the differences in performance between engaged and actively disengaged work units and found that those scoring in the top half on employee engagement nearly doubled their odds of success compared with those in the bottom half... If employees truly are a company's best asset, then their care and support should be a priority."

- Gallup

---

## CALL TO ACTION:

1. *START NOW - Today is the day to begin gaining a serious advantage over your competition. Not only will you stop wasting time, money, and effort on outdated or inefficient methods of gauging employee engagement, but you will also start to build the kind of irresistible organization so many others want to create.*

2. *TAKE OWNERSHIP - You, as the leadership or management of your company, have taken ownership of this issue. No longer willing to subcontract it out to a service provider, or to think of it as a once-each-year activity. You have chosen to make employee engagement a priority, putting it at the top of your to do list.*

3. *DEFINE The only way to ensure that all of these interactions are positive or beneficial is to clearly define employ-*

*ee engagement goals for your organization. Start thinking and talking about what you want to get out of employee engagement, what you expect to gain both personally, and for your organization.*

*Creating goals and direction for employee engagement is the focus of the next chapter. The important thing to take away from this one is that NOW is the moment you must turn your inefficient or poorly functioning employee engagement program on its head. When you do, you will become one of only a few innovative firms that mysteriously manage to thrive even in the new challenges of the Trust & Value Economy and the era of the employee as priority.*

# CHAPTER 6

## LOOKING INWARD – YOUR REALITY

How do you begin to adjust your employee engagement programs? Well, the good news is you already have: You have shifted your paradigm and gotten in the right frame of mind. Believe me, that is more than half the battle.

Naturally, that means that one of the key steps towards the creation of a solid employee engagement program is recognizing what that engagement is and what your program is meant to yield. Are you just looking for happy workers? Are you hoping to create a workplace with zero turnover? Perhaps you want high-quality production with zero defects in manufacturing. Perhaps, if you are like most leaders and CEOs, you want it all!

Your next step in creating a solid employee engagement plan is to step up to the plate and take ownership-of your employee engagement program. You need to take a long, hard look at your company and your current program, and gauge where you are in terms of clarity of purpose for your program

### CLARITY IS A KEY

When looking at your current program, take a long, hard look at the facts, and be realistic and honest. This is so important that I want to repeat it: It is important be honest with yourself about it. Is your employee engagement program getting the results you want? Could it be better? Is your program designed to ensure that you have clarified the results you want, and have you have put the strategies in place to make sure you achieve them?

Let's not overlook the obvious, you are an organization whose major goal is business success, and we know that to achieve success in this new economy, we need to grow and protect our greatest asset, our employees. That is the reason you need to clarify how you are going to ensure that strategy is executed and implemented.

For the most part, a business wants to be productive, profitable, and competitive. Let's just begin with that set of facts. Now, being competitive means having higher customer ratings and a stronger bottom line (among other things) than the others in your industry, or at least than most of them. To do that, to achieve that, understand you are dependent upon the level of engagement of your employees. To succeed at that level, you need employees who share that vision and care as much as you do about your business.

That is why it is important, first to get real. You need to determine how employees are or are not currently enabling your organization to be as profitable, productive, and competitive as you would like it to be. This varies widely from industry to industry and firm to firm, but engagement and performance are the most commonly intertwined in the following areas:

- ▶ Quality
- ▶ Turnover rate
- ▶ Safety (relating to customers and/or workers)
- ▶ Theft or loss
- ▶ Absenteeism

▸ Productivity

▸ Profitability

▸ Customer satisfaction/retention

The Gallup group indicates that there are "well-established connections between employee engagement" and those performance outcomes. For me, as a business strategist, this is strong information. Take a look at those areas again, and you will see that the level of engagement of your employees impacts every major area of success of your organization, which is great news if your team is fully engaged. We have some work to do if they are not.

Take a look at where you are in relation to these issues. Are you profitable as you want to be? Are you as productive as you could be? What are your customer ratings? How often are there problems relating to quality or defect? Are you positioned to maintain or grow in these areas going forward? You need a good understanding of where and how you rank in order to define and structure what you want your employee engagement program to accomplish.

Only you can gauge where you stand in these areas and where improvements must occur if your organization is to survive and thrive. I encourage you to go through this exercise and take an honest look at where you are and where you would like to be. Create a "current state" and a "desired state" for each area.

Once you recognize where employee disengagement is costing you in terms of outcomes, it is easier to begin formulating plans. Once you know what you want and need to improve, you can begin engaging your employees in how to get there.

## STRATEGIES FOR ENHANCING EMPLOYEE ENGAGEMENT

### Step One: Get to Know the Individual

I have to admit, I am not a fan of the job description. Oh, sure, it is a great outline, but I find it limiting in terms of individual growth and use of talents. People come to work with a personality and a set of personal needs and desires (even if they do not know it). They have talents, goals, beliefs, and backgrounds that are entirely unique. These are factors that drive or inhibit their performance in their job. They all have potential, but this can only be accessed when they are seen as more than what they do, or what they are supposed to do.

This is where leadership steps up and takes ownership of employee engagement. After all, how much of "who" a person is can be gauged by a standard employee engagement survey? On the other hand, a lot is gained when a manager or even a company leader takes the time to get to know the people around her. The manner in which leaders interact with employees always affects the way the employees engage in their jobs or workplace. This has an immediate impact on the success (or failure) of the company in meeting goals.

So, how focused are you on the individual? As a leader, do you take the time to get to know your employees, who they are, what strengths they bring to the table, and what they value or want from their career? Engaging employees begins with investing in them before you ask them to invest in you.

**Step Two: How Reactive Are You?**

This step asks you to take a look at your preexisting or—let's just say it—dysfunctional employee engagement programs and gauge just how reactive you are to the information received. Remember, you are not alone; a huge percentage of firms using engagement programs will collect data and then fail to do much, if anything, with it. For most organizations, employee engagement programs are nothing more than a process of going through the motions.

This may be because they just don't have the resources to do it, because they are not clear on what they can do with this information, or because they just don't have the infrastructure for making any real changes or responses. It is my experience that we are creatures of habit, and for some unknown reason we often fall victim to doing things one way simply because that is the way they have always been done.

Take this moment to consider your employee engagement program. You may have already realized that you are not collecting relevant or actionable data. You might see that you just have not laid the groundwork for effective action, or that your results (the point of doing the program) never seem to get better.

Always keep in mind that emphasizing the employee as an individual will require that you act on any information you receive. Asking for opinions demands that you, at the very least, respond; not doing so will undermine any positive feeling you created by asking for feedback in the first place. Even just responding makes a huge difference. Always remember people want and need to be heard.

If the modern business model has to be transparent, then the data collected needs to be freely shared. Letting people know the results of surveys is important, and being willing and able to act on the findings is the next step. Naturally, this also means your leadership, at all levels, should be open to all feedback and be fully engaged and ready to respond as well.

So how prepared are you to hear real feedback, and how prepared are you to take any actionable steps?

### Step Three: Do You Have the Right Leadership In Place?

Whether you are prepared to take action or not, this is a time to determine if you have leadership in place that can handle the shift into this new paradigm.

As one expert indicated, "Real change occurs at the local workgroup level," and that demands that the leadership and management be solid (Gallup.com). Leaders have the biggest impact on whether change happens and is sustainable when it comes to fully engaging employees.

"Leaders and managers should work with employees to identify barriers to engagement and opportunities to effect positive change," says the Gallup report, and to achieve this goal, you need to have the right leaders in place.

Not everyone can be a good leader or manager. As you make the shift, you need to first put a lot of effort into assessing management. Ask some pointed questions of current management:

▸ Does a manager look at employees as individuals with unique strengths, and see the need to use those strengths?

▸ Is a manager someone with a proven record for empowering others? For instance, does she seek and listen to ideas and opinions? Does she value and recognize the contributions of others?

▸ Does the manager view the employees as the force behind the company's success as well as his own?

▸ Are they open to being held accountable for the level at which their team is engaged?

These criteria are part of what will make a manager effective where the employee is concerned.

Not all companies can easily identify such individuals among their ranks, and that could mean that you have to initiate a search for appropriate "local level" leadership from within your existing pool of employees. In addition, think about investing in the training of your supervisors and managers, helping them understand what employee engagement is and why it is critical to the success of your organization.

**Step Four: Are You Willing to Coach?**

Regardless of whether you have solid management or the need to recruit from within, you also have to determine if you are willing to establish a coaching-like component to the roles of managers and leaders. When writing a white paper on employee engagement, the presence of a strong coaching program was one of the major strategies CEOS listed as a strong indicator for long-term success of employee engagement programs.

Coaching is critical on so many levels to the success of any employee engagement program. It is defined as a way of helping others to discover themselves, their talents, and their skills, and a way to ensure they develop, learn new skills, achieve goals, and so on. It can be seen as a form of focused engagement, as it requires leaders to communicate and connect with their employees, and, unlike training or mentoring, it requires employees (coachees) to provide input and ideas to their leaders (coaches). Thereby letting the coachee, not the leader, run the show.

In short, managers need to be coached in order to succeed in the active role of managing employee engagement goals and initiatives. And employees need to be coached as a way to continually and consistently engage them. After all, if we are truly to turn the employee engagement model on its head, managers and employees have to talk and listen rather than just fill out surveys.

For years, we have told our leaders to learn to listen to customers, take an interest in them, and build relationships. The coaching process allows us as leaders to do the very same thing with our employees. To put together a successful employee engagement program, managers will have to be fully engaged in knowing their people, listening to their ideas, helping them to reach goals, tracking new varieties of "progress," and keeping close watch over all of their employees' levels of engagement. For many, this is also an entirely new way of managing and a very different style of leadership.

**Step Five: Is Everything Clear and in Realistic Terms?**

Earlier, we looked at the issue of clarity and the need to define your goals. Let's revisit that, because it is so important to success and needs to be done as completely as possible. Begin by taking a very sharp look at the terminology you are using and the goals you feel you should set.

If employee engagement is to become a living, organic part of your business strategy, the goals of the program have to mean something to employees, not just emphasize business goals.

For example, author Edward Lawler pointed out that "money does not motivate performance"; profit-sharing plans or other similar "carrot and stick" programs may seem like ways of reaching business goals (i.e. profit levels), but they are not keys to employee engagement.

While bonuses and perks are nice, what truly engages employees are clearly defined and well communicated expectations. For instance, being able to describe "what success looks like" in a language that appeals emotionally to the employee allows them to connect to that success, and will build commitment exponentially. When you define it, they can visualize it and see themselves becoming it.

Remember that in the previous chapters I pointed out that employees need to feel they are part of something bigger than they are, or to have an experience more than a "career." Given that, you need to design employee engagement goals to create and inspire a sense of purpose for your employees.

"Alignment" is a frequently used term, and it can happen when managers and employees are able to connect what they do to the vision of the organization. When that level of alignment happens, a solid step of engagement occurs. When the goals are phrased in such a way as to become part of the organization's lexicon, best practices, and/or daily interactions between management and workers, the strategy becomes a living thing.

## IN THEIR OWN WORDS...

Author Judy McLeish has this to say about overcoming the problems inherent in traditional engagement: "Design an approach to engage your entire senior leadership team, as well as your frontline managers. In order to create leaders who are both engaged themselves and who are able to foster engagement, you'll need to create an approach that provides them the training and tools to drive engagement. Remember, engagement is a journey – it won't happen overnight, so ensure that the approach has the appropriate milestones to show progress against the plan."

## CALL TO ACTION:

1. *Commit to making the shift, and begin the process by asking yourself these questions::*

   *Where will you need to focus as you make the shift from your traditional employee engagement approaches to this new model?*

   *Where are you right now, in terms of getting to know and building relationships with your employees as individuals?*

   *How do you look beyond job descriptions and see potential in your employees?*

   *How do you help managers to navigate this shift? How do you help them to measure and respond to employee engagement issues?*

2. *Create solid, workable, and clear goals around what you want from an engaged workforce, and what difference it will make.*

3. *Lastly, and most importantly you need to keep your focus inward. Remember a solid employee engagement program begins with you, the leader. Your actions will do more to determine the success of your program more than anything else. When you assess how you are doing with each of these steps, you can consistently work to improve your employee engagement skills, and with that, the team will follow.*

*As you discover just where to focus in order to make a shift to your new paradigm, you have to rely on existing resources. Where and what are they? The next chapter continues this inward look at the team and the company, and how you can rebuild foundations from the resources and programs you currently have in place.*

# CHAPTER 7

## A NEW PERSPECTIVE

We all know the very definition of insanity is doing the same thing repeatedly and expecting a different result. Yet ever year, many of us look at our employee engagement programs and agree on some level that these expensive and complicated programs are not working only to sign up for and repeat the same process all over again, expecting better results.

If you really want to shift your employee engagement program, you have to begin with you. The fastest and most permanent way to get things to change is to begin with you If you want things to change, then you need to change. You need to try new things, and approach employee engagement from a different perspective. In other words, you need to shift your paradigm. If you do not begin by looking at employee engagement from a different perspective, you will simply build the same model or program you have always built. To change your employee engagement program, you need to change the way you see, think about, and view employee engagement.

Creating a truly effective employee engagement program begins with accepting that any employee engagement program you build will never be good enough. Okay, that may be an overstatement, but my point is that in order to be effective, your program needs to be in a constant state of review. We are living in a shifting economy, meaning that any plan or strategy that is effective today may not work as well a few months from now. You need to be open to keeping your plan updated and adjusted to ensure the best results. It is time to commit to a new approach, one that involves risk, courage, and the admission that you may not have all the answers.

Now, the solution is simple just shift your paradigm. How hard can that be, right? Well actually shifting, as opposed to just saying it, turns out is not that easy. Luckily for us, employee engagement is a hot topic, and new statistics and measurements come out daily, reinforcing that what we have been doing is just not getting the job done.

With rampant change being the new way we do business, again we have to look at employee engagement as a key part of our business strategy, something executive level leaders focus on and hold themselves accountable for. That right there is a major paradigm shift.

As we have discussed before, employee engagement has always taken a back seat to things like budgeting, strategy, and sales. Walk into any boardroom and you would hear leaders discuss many issues, but rarely, if ever, would you hear a long discussion about employee engagement or the programs being put in place to retain top talent. Let me take that back, you may hear this issue discussed, but not the commitment or accountability to solve the issue at the leadership level.

If you want employees to engage, then the buck needs to stop with you as the leader. What you focus on as the CEO of the company, what you care about, is what your next level leaders and key associates will care about. If you give employee engagement lip service, so will they. If you focus on it, put passion and energy into it, so will they. It is that important and requires that level of focus. This is a long journey, and you need to be the guide. -

In the last chapter, we touched on refining just what employee engagement means within your organization, and how directly connected your business goals and performance are to the level of engagement of your employees.

It was at this point that I asked you to do some serious assessments on where you stand on issues like individuality, your readiness to take actionable steps from surveys or engagement programs, accountability at all leadership levels, your willingness to "coach", and how clear you are in your communications of expectations and goals. You were asked to describe what success looks like in terms of employee engagement, and to determine how to align your goals with your strategies. You now should have the clearest portrait of what employee engagement means to your firm or organization, and what it means to you.

If you are anything like many of today's modern employers, though, you may find that your ideal is not the reality. The goal you want to achieve is far your current state. You don't need precise percentages garnered from detailed engagement surveys. You know already, you just have to look at your pool of employees to know that your program and your team are not where you want and need them to be.

So let's jump into this and walk through the steps you should take to prepare to turn things around, shake them up, and build the program you want.

Readjusting Your Perspective

## THE REAL WORLD

*I was speaking at an event in Chicago, Illinois, and was blessed to share the stage with a dynamic leader who was speaking that day on customer service. Her angle was a little different than most who speak on the subject. She was speaking on service from the perspective of the impact leadership and employee engagement have on our customers.*

*She was sharing a story about the connection of engagement and service, explaining that if your employees are not engaged, you need to first look to the leader. While there may be many reasons or justifications for why your employee engagement program is not top notch, the only true reason is because the leader does not "own" the problem. If the leader passes the buck, any program, no matter how good, falls apart. She went on to explain that today, in our corporate environments, passing the buck has become commonplace, as we have all fallen victim to the "corporate salute." With that, she gave us an example of the corporate salute, folding her arms and pointing in both directions, then explained to the audience that the corporate salute is pointing the finger and blaming someone else when accountability comes your way.*

*We have become an outward-facing society, looking first for someone else to pass the buck to, point a finger at, or blame when something goes wrong. And when it comes to creating an effective employee engagement program, the "corporate salute" just will not work.*

*For the most part, the trend is to look outward. I call it the "blame them" mentality, rather than blaming yourself, and while it may be fun to blame other people, it is completely ineffective. The mindset that "if they..." pointing towards employees as the reason that engagement fails. Again, while it may be fun, heck it could even be true, the problem is it does not work, nothing changes when you focus blame on others.*

*To build a solid foundation, you have to look inward—at yourself, your leadership team, and your organization. Take a long, hard, honest look and admit what you see: the strengths, the challenges, and the opportunities. This inward scrutiny gauges what sort of resources and impediments you have as you prepare to make major changes at every level. After all, you cannot implement change effectively if you do not have the manpower and framework for doing so. You cannot build a foundation if there are no bricks and mortar, and if you don't know where the skeletons are buried.The best way to build a solid foundation from the bottom up is to begin by looking from the top down!*

## THE REAL WORLD

*The partners of HORNE LLP, a highly successful southeast regional accounting firm headquartered in Mississippi, embraced a vision of building the Wise firm (a concept and movement that will be highlighted throughout this book). They realized the perfect storm was brewing in public accounting; the storm was already raging offshore, with high demand for talent, colliding generational differences, unprecedented succession gaps, and failure of traditional ideas to meet the changing needs of the workforce. Outdated strategies lacked the ability to inspire greatness among team members, with problems including lack of flexibility, stringent top-down communications, sink-or-swim leadership development, and lack of vision and purpose. The partners at HORNE knew that business as usual was no longer an option for them and that they must prepare for the coming storm.*

*Rather than looking outward to hire consultants and experts, which is what we as professionals are conditioned and programmed to do, they turned inward to solve the problem. Led by HORNE Executive Partner Joey Havens, the partners at HORNE began the process by peeling back the layers on their current engagement programs and people management systems and taking a very honest look into what was working and what was not. By all industry standards and points of measurement, the bottom line, the competition, and firm growth, HORNE was doing exceptionally well and was considered a leader in their field.*

*Although change is difficult when things are going well, HORNE realized they wanted to define who they would be in the future. To be a great firm, what they were doing would not take them forward. As Joey Havens studied the future of the profession, he saw the changing landscape and knew HORNE was not ready, not doing enough. He knew they were not doing enough to not only remain a leader but, more importantly, to be the type of firm they wanted to become. So their journey began there, by getting a very real and bare-bones look at the state of the company and the profession, and by defining clearly what it would take to become the firm they wanted to be.*

## NO "I" IN TEAM... NO "US AND THEM"

When it comes to employee engagement, there should be no "us" versus "them." For the effort to work, you have to agree—before you even start—that collaboration and compromise are the only true ways to get there.

However, before we delve into the many key points of making a paradigm shift, it is important that you understand that it is not an "either/or" or an "us or them" venture—it is everyone. While we will look at it from a "top-down" perspective, with a tremendous portion of responsibility firmly in the hands of leadership, your employees will always be a major part of the picture too, and everyone must take their share of responsibility.

The term "inclusion" often appears, subtly, in articles and books focused on best practices in new employee engagement, but it is a powerful word, and I want to draw attention to it. Inclusion, for our discussion, means involving your team, making them a part of the process, and engaging employee as a shared practice. After all, this is a paradigm shift, and keeping employees separate from something as relevant to them as employee engagement policies is precisely how we got in this mess in the first place.

Step one in your paradigm shift is to see this as a dual role, with shared responsibility. To truly engage employees, you need traditional top-down leadership working with a grassroots employee effort that produces a new type of product, a new type of employee, and a new type of company.

If you want to engage employees from the bottom up, you have to begin from the top down!

## BUILDING A FOUNDATION

So why do you even need a foundation for an employee engagement structure? Because in order for it to withstand the constant pace of change, the obstacles it will hit, and the challenges it needs to overcome, it needs to be rooted in something solid and strong. If you are to be successful in redefining your entire approach to employee engagement, you need to be certain of your footing.

A strong foundation comes down to two things: your corporate values and your leadership, in that order. I wrote a lot about values in Winning in the Trust & Value Economy, and while I felt that values have always been an important part of business success, in today's economy they are critical for success.

Clearly articulated and well-communicated values ensure that you, everyone who works with you, and your customers understand exactly who you are, what you stand for, and what they can expect when doing business or working with you. Values are your guideposts, the very touchpoints you check in with when setting goals, making decisions, and hiring and promoting team members.

Values are your foundation; if you are not actively using your values, then your foundation is shaky. When companies and leaders are aligned with their values, they create and build trust, two very important pieces of the employee engagement process.

## WHY COMMITMENT AS A VALUE MATTERS

Once you clearly articulate and align with your values, you are well on your way to a solid, authentic employee engagement program. From there, you can hire, choose customers, develop partnerships, and promote leaders who align with, live, and personify your values.

Leadership is the next key piece in building a solid foundation. Gallup's State of the American Workplace Report for 2013 says, "Looking at employee engagement through the lens of the employee, their leader or direct supervisor has great impact on how and why they choose or do not choose to engage."

Leadership is a powerful force in why and how employees engage, and if you want to get serious about employee engagement, you need to get serious about leadership. Every leader on your team needs to be chosen first for their values, their alignment of values with your organizations, and then for their experience.

We have all seen it far too often: the company listing their values as one thing, only to have leaders who care about an lead with an entirely different set of values. You will see company values saying things like, "We put our customers and our employees first," only to have a leader unable to remember the last time he scheduled a coaching session or spent some one-on-one time with a team member.

The moment that the leader does not align his actions with the the values of the company, there is a crack in your employee engagement program. The misalignment sends a confusing message and creates a level of uncertainty or mistrust, which undermines engagement.

## OUTSIDE INFLUENCE: THE OTHER DRIVERS OF EMPLOYEE ENGAGEMENT

While alignment of values and leaders are critical to success of your employee engagement program, there are more drivers, outside influences, that have a significant impact on the level to which your employees engage.

We often think of employee engagement in terms of a smaller picture—the people they work with, whom they report to, and whether or not they like their job. It is actually quite bigger than that; there are four areas that have direct impact on the level to which your employees will or will not engage.

According to the CEB HR Leadership Council, employees engage when they feel committed to their job, manager, team, and organization. The more connected and committed your associates feel to all four areas, the more likely it is you will retain them while simultaneously seeing an increase in performance.

## FOUR TYPES OF COMMITMENT IN AN ORGANIZATION/BUSINESS

- ▶ Commitment to Team – The amount your employees enjoy working with their co-workers, and the extent to which they feel the team's work matters and is important.

- ▶ Commitment to Manager – The level to which their manager can and is willing to advance their career, and the extent to which they believe their manager advances their skills and knowledge.

  - ▶ When an employee is committed to both of these areas (team and manager), you will see an increase in his overall performance.

- ▶ Commitment to Job – The extent to which employees enjoy their jobs and day-to-day work, and the extent to which they feel their jobs challenge and develop them.

- ▶ Commitment to Organization – Whether or not employees share the same values as the organization, and the extent to which they buy into their organization's culture.

When employees are committed to their job and organization, you have a higher chance of retaining them over the long term. And commitment to all four of these areas ensures you have not only a highly performing team, but one that is committed to stay with your company long-term.

Until I came across this research, I did not fully understand why I chose to leave corporate America. At the time, I was at the top of my game, having come off a series of successful years, and was positioned to be promoted to a top job. I loved my boss, and I would have followed him to the ends of the earth, and I was crazy about my team.

I was, however, bored with my job and what I was doing day in and day out, and even the thought of a promotion did not hold much appeal. Somewhere along the line, I had lost my belief in the company goals and what we were trying to accomplish long-term. I no longer felt committed to job or my organization.

So while I may have held two of the four kinds of commitment— commitment to my team and to my boss—a lack of faith in my company and my boredom with my job caused me to no longer be engaged and seek employment elsewhere.

So how do you get your employees to commit and engage with all four areas, so you create not only a high-performing team, but one that you can retain long-term?

Well, that takes a full circle back to values and leadership.

While having values and strong leaders is one thing, communicating that is another. Communication, when it comes to employee engagement, is really about clarity and understanding.

Clarity that leaders know what they expect and want from their employees, and clarity that employees understand what is expected of them. Clarity of company vision and how they, as employees, fit into that, and how they can help to accomplish the goal. In order for full engagement to happen, employees need to be as clear about the direction of the organization as leadership is.

So what does a leader in today's engaged employee culture look like? We all know the traditional skills and characteristics of a great leader, qualities such as courage, honesty, and the willingness to take a risk, but to truly lead a team that fully engages it takes more.

Entrepreneur created a unique list of qualities, worth reviewing and thinking about if you want to fully engage today's employees. Successful leaders today must:

- Give employees something to reach for.
- Embody the company vision.
- Create and be involved in company culture (i.e. connect).
- Rely on transparency.
- Protect morale at all times.

When you have a leader who both has and acts on these qualities, hold onto him and work with him to help other leaders acquire these skills. In addition, you need to look beyond your leadership team to find those employees non-leadership roles with these same assets. You have them, trust me, you do, and if you want to fully engage employees, you need to learn to recognize leadership at every level and give those leaders space to lead, whether or not they are in formal leadership roles.

To turn your employee engagement program on its head, to create a program that is highly successful, you need all the leadership resources you can get, and all the leadership resources throughout every level of your organization.

While your willingness to begin integrating the components of effective engagement is an essential part of the process, it is just a first step at assessing resources. These new steps or patterns (recognizing the leaders, taking action, establishing clarity, etc.) are just a part of your "new" resources.

Resources also include the managers and leadership that you have in place, and whether or not they are able to make the change, whether they can own their part of employee engagement changes.

And this is where we get to the crux of the matter—owning it. Engagement can just as easily translate to ownership, the mental "stepping up to the plate" that is required to implement a paradigm shift.

The analogy of stepping up to the plate is ideal, because it demonstrates all of the points at which we are looking. The individual knows the expectations, she understands the value of her role in the greater scheme of things (the team, success, and so on), and she engages fully by owning that responsibility and actively doing all she can do what it takes to knock it out of the park. Now that is engagement, but it is also a great portrait of how empowering it can be to experience ownership.

When we talk about how empowering ownership is, how personally powerful it is to experience ownership, we are really getting to the purpose of this book, this idea of redefining responsibility. That means seeing responsibility not as a burden but as your opportunity to move into a position of control in your own career, success, and overall happiness.

## THE DOMINO IMPACT OF ENGAGEMENT

This inward assessment may make it painfully clear that your organization is already at risk for providing employees with one of those three "causes" for disengagement (inadequate training or a lack of development opportunities, seriously disproportionate earnings, or the wrong leadership).

For example, you might look at one of your frontline managers and see that you have a high performer, a go-getter, but that this go-getter does not exhibit the company values, or is not the slightest bit interested in developing her team. Even if this manager exceeds her goals and performs highly, she may exhibit qualities that actually undermine other employees' motivation to engage.

This is one of the hardest paradigm shifts for executive leadership to make, to understand that leadership, at every level, is critical to the overall success of any employee engagement program. And just because an employee is a top performer (according to your old measurements of performance) does not mean they should be a leader or a evne a member of your team.

When I worked in the banking industry, this very issue was a constant problem. With only vertical promotion opportunities, top performers (those who could produce, but showed not skill in the areas of leadership) were often taken out of producing roles and moved into positions of leadership. In addition, top performers who routinely brought in business that was questionable or did not match the values and expectations of the bank were rewarded with awards and accolades.

Again, this is a tough paradigm shift to make, but you need to understand the  negative impact this has on employee engagement and why without solving this issue your employees will continue to disengage.

A leader who does not have a passion for engaging employees is a leader who is negatively impacting those he is leading. A top performer who brings in business is an asset, but not one you need to necessarily promote to a leader of people. If he does not have values that clearly align with the values of the company, it sends a mixed message to both employees and customers alike. It creates a long-term problem for the company that undoes all the good and, perhaps the profit he brought into the company in the first place.

The only way to have an effective employee engagement program, one that encourages your team to step up to the plate, take ownership, and drive results, is to put the right leaders in the right positions.

## YOUR MANAGEMENT RESOURCES

The keys to a successful employee engagement program are awareness and responsibility, at both the leadership and the employee level. While it has to begin from the top down, it will never be sustainable if it is not driven from the bottom up. Employee engagement is described in so many different ways, but the bottom line is that it is emotional. Employee engagement is something people feel, and something they are internally motivated to do. When an employee is engaged he makes a connection and an emotional attachment to their job, their organization, their team and their leader. An employee who has that level of connection is fully engaged.

When choosing leaders, you need people who embrace and understand that engagement is emotional, not something you can force on somebody, and your leaders need to understand and be committed to creating a culture where those who want to emotionally connect (engage) can.

As writer Peter Stark said, "True employee engagement is internal; it cannot be forced, and it cannot be bought. To create a workplace of excellence in which top talent has the ability to thrive, managers need to take responsibility for not only the engagement of their employees, but also their own engagement."

Emotional connection begins with a relationship, and to have a relationship we need to get to know our employees; leaders need to invest in learning who their employees are, who they are and what they care about. Business journalist Robyn Reilly wrote a piece that describes this idea perfectly:

Though important at the organizational level, engagement starts with each person and is subjective... Each person's potential extends well beyond his or her job description. And tapping that potential means recognizing how an employee's unique set of beliefs, talents, goals, and life experiences drives his or her performance. Managers and leaders should know who their people are, not just what they do.

## IN THEIR OWN WORDS...

TAICO Incentive Services says that there are "golden keys" to engaging your workforce, and summarizes it thusly:

"This is the golden key.

Can you answer the following questions in the affirmative?

Are you recognizing your employees' small wins? Does your workplace provide a safe haven to present new ideas and take risks? Do your employees feel that their dignity is being protected and their voices heard? Do you recognize and reward real progress?

Understanding how to use this golden key will reduce employee turnover and boost your overall employee performance."

- TAICO, 2015

So you have to ask yourself: Have you set this tone? Does your organization support this, and have you, as a leader yourself, done the work to truly get to know and connect with your team members? Millennials will eventually comprise the vast majority of the workforce, and it is precisely this sort of feedback and engagement they require to experience job satisfaction and, more importantly, to engage.

No matter our age, generation, or background, being part of community matters to us, and it is critical in the employee engagement process. Leaders need to understand that to fully engage your team, you need to go beyond ensuring people understand their job and their role. Leaders need to go beyond and take the step to invest in their team, learn about them, and care about them as people and individuals first.

Fully engaging people is about creating a leader who shares clarity of vision, roles, and responsibility, and invests in committing to his team before he asks his team to invest in him. So begin building your foundation there, taking stock of the leaders you have in place and ensuring that you have invested in getting everyone on the same page, and that everything is in alignment.

With leadership all working from the same model, you have built half the foundation you need for a strong employee engagement program. Now it is time to change your focus to the employee. Today's employee engagement programs often leave out one very important part of the process, one very key piece of the foundation: the employee.

## YOUR EMPLOYEE RESOURCES

Who are your employees? Do you have a grasp of who they are and what is important to them? What makes them tick, what makes them a good fit, and what makes motivates them to commit to your organization? To have an effective employee engagement program, you need to begin by taking inventory of your current employee resources.

After all, employees are the engine of your organization; the only way to make change is to understand what needs to change, and only your employees know the answer to that.

The old method of managers and leaders coming together in a closed setting, like a boardroom or retreat, to discuss employee engagement is an unworkable, "at a distance" approach. Engagement can be quite simple, if you just directly ask employees to convey to you the "things" that are causing them to disengage. Surveys are great, but local level leadership and committed managers are the ones who uncover the real roadblocks and create the trust and relationships that it takes to make real change.

Directly engaging employees in both uncovering the problem and creating the solution creates inclusion and transparency that tells employees their voice matters. Directly engaging (asking, listening, and taking action) creates ownership at every level, to get results at every turn.

This is the heart of engagement, and it allows you, as a leader, to inventory your resources within your entire team, and then integrate them into the process as you enter this transformational time.

## CALL TO ACTION

1. *Build the Foundation - Begin laying the foundation for change by performing an inward, organizational assessment. What sort of resources do you have on hand? What does your existing leadership bring to the table, and what are they missing?*

2. *Honest Self-Assessment – Again be open, honest, and unbiased in your assessment. Really look at your leaders and team, and gauge their alignment with your values.*

3. *Engaged in Engagement - Once you have built a fully committed leadership team, it is time to take it to the employees. Again, go in and assess which team members "get it", which do not, and strive to understand why. Is it a leadership issue? A values issue? A communication issue?*

4. *Leadership Matters - Understand that to build a solid foundation you first need the "right" leaders, those who are bought into and role model your vision, mission, and values. You need leaders who are willing to share the role of creating this program equally with employees—who embrace the idea that the only way to truly engage employees is by building a program that is driven simultaneously from the top down and from the bottom up. If you have the right leadership in place great. If not, it is time to take action.*

# CHAPTER 8

## THE MARRIAGE OF LEADER & EMPLOYEE

This is an economy in which relationships rule, and the relationships you build with your employees are just as, if not more important than the relationships you build with your customers.

I am not promoting the adages that say, "The employee is always right" or, "We would have no business without our employees." However, when you look at employees with the same lens through which you view customers, you'll find a lot of useful insight. For example, great customer service involves asking a lot of questions, listening, and investing in getting to know them before we ask them to get to know us. While great for customer service, I would say it is a strategy that works great for employees too.

Simply changing your view and depth of relationships with employees helps you begin to see them as the valuable assets they are, and sheds some light on why the current process of how we work with them needs some work. When, in the process of engagement, you get your employees involved through asking questions, gathering input, and listening, you give them a voice and role, and with that role comes ownership of both the process and the solution.

An employee engagement program designed with the input of all involved is one that becomes much easier to get everyone to "own," to take responsibility for its success.

Now that idea sounds a little easier than it actually is, as creating a culture where ideas flow top-down and bottom-up, I find one of the biggest obstacles is fear. Fear of change, of what might be said or shared and of being pushed outside of your comfort zone.

Fear is a small word with a powerful impact and has probably been more responsible for shutting down good ideas, lowering moral, and disengaging bright, imaginative, and talented employees than anything else. So I want to say this and make it clear: It is better not to ask for feedback, not to ask for your team's ideas and opinions, if you do not really want to hear it, or if you are not going to take action.

## RESPONSIBILITY AND AWARENESS

Employee engagement programs fail for a combination of reasons, but two of the most important are that your employees do not feel connected, and that they understand their priorities. In order to engage, employees need to feel that they belong and that their job makes a difference. More than sixty percent of employee discipline issues can be traced back to lack of clarity. Simply put, employees are focusing on the wrong things, performing their jobs incorrectly, or failing to carry out policies and procedures only because they are not clear on what you as the leader need or most want from them. Your job as a leader is to help ensure that all team members understand, at all levels, the overall vision and their role in it. It is important that every member of your team is sure what it is they are meant to engage with, what they can do to help accomplish that vision, or even what rewards are gained by making the effort.

Just the step of communicating the vision and creating awareness will begin to shift, for the positive, the level to which your employees will engage. I fundamentally believe that people come to work wanting to contribute, to excel in their role, and to be part of a winning team. You just need to ensure they understand how.

## IN THEIR OWN WORDS...

"To build a common understanding of the engagement goal, discuss it during team impact-planning meetings and in one-on-one feedback sessions with employees. For example, if your goal is to boost recognition among your team members, ask them, 'What would we need to do for everyone on the team to strongly agree that "in the last seven days, I have received recognition or praise for doing good work"? What would it take for you to give this item a top score?'"

- Knight, 2015

Now, awareness is not just about the company's success or what the organization is trying to accomplish; while that is important, you also need to make employees aware of what is in it for them. In the new economy, employees need to understand that a direct benefit of employee engagement is the power they have when they take personal ownership of their own engagement. Sure, the company is going to win, but the true payoff when an employee makes the decision to engage is for them.

### TAKING OWNERSHIP

Think about the words and phrases that you can associate with the concept of ownership: responsibility, freedom, control, personal power, benefits. These concepts lead to thoughts of purpose, motivation, and results.

As one study said, "Only 24% of people can link what they do on a daily basis to the Key Results of the organization." Only 24%—wow! And that means if they do not understand how their work impacts the success of the company, they cannot begin to connect how doing their job well could help them personally.

When people cannot make the connection to advancing the cause of the organization, or understand why their job and role matters, they become less invested and less enthused with fulfilling the purpose of the organization. Seventy-four percent of business executives feel that the Key Results their organization needs to achieve are not clearly understood throughout the organization and, therefore, not being actively pursued."

As the leader, it is your responsibility to create that awareness, your responsibility to make sure that key results are clear, and ensure that employees understand how their effort connects to the company's success. This creates common understanding of and confidence in where the organization is headed. It ensures awareness of the expectations of all involved, and the benefits of shared community, as everyone has a role and together you achieve success.

As leaders who want to create powerful employee engagement programs, we need to redefine how we view, and how our employees see, ownership and responsibility. We need to "change" the definition (of responsibility) from "burden" or "obligation" to "freedom" and "purpose." Taking responsibility, being willing to play your part and commit to the role, is the first step in securing ownership, ensuring you have a voice and are heard.

## DEFINING OWNERSHIP

Individual ownership is very powerful stuff!

Ownership should be seen as "the ability to tie where you are with what you have done and where you want to be with what you are going to do" (OzPrinciple.org, 2015). This goes way beyond a basic list of responsibilities, roles, and awareness. It means you are taking charge, and you have the control to take on challenges, overcome obstacles, and achieve opportunities.

In fact, ownership is the key to individual employees and the entire company moving past having goals, to becoming an organization and a team creating transformational change.

Of course, if you cannot "tie" what you want to be to the place where you are going, that means you do not have vision. Remember, without vision you cannot provide your team with the clarity they need to fully engage. There are four distinct steps that add up to a very clear outcome, to ensure you can understand, communicate, and ultimately inspire your team to OWN IT!

The four steps are:

1. Personally investing in the situation.
2. Recognizing your role.
3. Working at all times on alignment.
4. Recognizing and dedicating yourself to your team and personal objectives.

This checklist is actually a roadmap to exactly how to lay the groundwork for creating a culture to inspire ownership.

## THE ROLES AND OWNING THEM

But before we can inspire our leaders and our teams to take ownership, we need to understand where people are on the scale, what the starting point is.

Its hard to believe, but some workers are not even aware of their disengagement, because they do not have good role models, or do not work inside a culture that asks for or creates awareness of what engagement even is. If the leader does not set the stage, it is understandable that the employee may not realize the expectation or see that they are not meeting it.

One exercise you can do as a leader, to get a general feel for how engaged your team is, is to assess them. Assess them in a very simple, easy manner that gives you a good overall understanding of where each member of your team sits on the engagement ladder. Set some time aside to sit down with a few other members of your leadership team, with a full list of your employees, and then decide, based on these four categories, into which category each employee falls.

1. Resistant - This is the lowest category and features those who do not recognize a need to be changed, or who resist doing anything differently.

2. Exempt - This is a level of ownership in which teams or employees agree that change is needed but often say it is change that applies to others, not to themselves.

3. Compliant - This is a level in which there can be some disengagement, though action is out of a sense of duty. Often those with ownership at this level lack what is needed to get to the desired outcome.

4. Invested – As the highest level, this is born of a group agreeing and participating fully; "hearts and minds" are fully engaged, and everyone understands the benefits to be gained by full investment.

(OzPrinciple.org, 2015)

Doing this will answer the questions you need to ask as a leader: How much of your team is engaged and takes ownership? How many of them even understand the concept, or are aware they should be engaged? What percentage is invested? This is a great way to get a baseline feel for where each of your employees are on the engagement scale.

Let's assume every member of your team puts her hands to work daily with intent of "working" hard, but without a concept of ownership their commitment can be misdirected or lose momentum. The more you understand has a leader how to inspire their ownership (i.e. hearts and minds, as well as hands) the more productive, efficient and fully engaged team you will have.

Making this happen requires (and begins with) understanding how engaged each member of your team is, and then creating a culture that inspires or offers each employee an opportunity to more fully engage.

When leadership creates a culture of ownership, then the job of leading the company becomes a joint venture, a 50/50 shared responsibility between employee and leader, each understanding that their success is connected and interdependent.

## THE REAL WORLD

*Consider the story of Rackspace (the IT hosting firm). Their mission is "fanatical customer support." Their top performers are rewarded with special recognition known as a Straightjacket, awarded monthly. This is, in their world, the highest honor that any team member—or "Racker," as they call them—can receive. It is awarded to the Racker who goes above and beyond, and who is fanatical about customer service.*

*As a payoff to the firm, they have some of the highest customer loyalty in their industry, and growth that has exceeded 50% in less than a decade.*

## HOW IS IT DONE? BAIN.COM SAYS:

Rackspace invests heavily in nurturing a culture of employee engagement through regular team meetings with supervisors and by organizing cross-functional teams around customers. Many companies with highly engaged employees like Rackspace take an approach that insists supervisors talk often with their teams to solicit feedback, identify the root causes of their concerns and then follow through with meaningful changes to the work environment and processes in which work gets done.

In other words, leaders work with their employees to decide how best to deliver that service, what it should be, and how to ensure it is exceptional. Everyone in the company is clear on what they need to do, everyone in the company has a say in how it is done, and everyone in the company is responsible for ensuring it happens.

When the right culture is created, with the right leaders leading, then it is only natural that the right employees step to the plate. They begin caring about the company as much as you do, and, in doing so, transfer that experience to your customers.

## CALL TO ACTION:

1. *Assess yourself and ensure that you have communicated what engagement and true ownership are, and what the personal and company benefits are of being engaged?" In other words, explain the "why" of what you are doing to your team, and why it matters.*

2. *Ensure your engaged leadership team is engaged correctly. That they are grounded in the basics: vision, mission, values, and role clarity.*

3. *Then assess your team on their level of awareness of the concept, their understanding of how to do it, and their initiative to take action. Determine the level to which you can and need to invite them to take ownership, or, just like with your leaders, move on and find them a seat on someone else's bus.*

*With the above complete, you will be in the position to begin to create an employee ownership program that is a joint venture between leadership and employee—a program that inspires ownership at every level and results at every turn.*

# CHAPTER 9

## YOUR RETURN ON INVESTMENT (ROI)

The beauty of employee engagement is that, as a leader, when you do the right thing, invest in and care about your employees, they do the right things for you. The results of leaders and employees working together and becoming a fully engaged team are increased bottom-line results and decreased workplace stress; in other words, there is a strong return on investment (ROI).

### THE REAL WORLD

*David Long, CEO of MyEmployees.com, built his company around his belief that if you do the right thing, live to your values, invest in your team and your customers, and treat people well, the business will grow—and grow it has.*

*In a time when businesses are struggling to keep from losing market share, David's business has and continues to grow. Last year, the company's earnings improved by 46% over the year before, a number that means so much more than "earnings" to David:*

*"I believe the only true way to grow a business and sustain that growth in this economy is through employee engagement.*

*But understand the bottom line growth is only part of the picture; leading and working with a fully engaged team makes work so much less like work. Your people are happy, the innovation is constant, and the job of growth and results is a shared responsibility, making the burden of business growth, not really a burden."*

*So what is the return on investment from an engaged workforce? Why does it matter, what improves? Well, let's begin by looking at what it is costing you NOT to have an engaged workforce, not to reinvent how you lead and how you hire.*

## THE COST OF DISENGAGEMENT

According to research performed and published by McLean & Company, there is a significant negative impact to your bottom line results when you leave employee engagement out of your business strategy. According to McLean & Company:

▸ Just one disengaged employee costs an organization approximately $3,400 for every $10,000 in annual salary.

▸ Disengaged employees cost the American economy up to $450 billion per year due to the lack of an engaged team.

▸ So the path to profitability in this Trust & Value Economy is through the relationships built with and the engagement level of your employees.

So let's look at the good news: What improves, and what can you expect when you invest both time and resources in engaging your team?

In research published in the report Engaging for Success: Enhancing Performance through Employee Engagement,, researchers David Mac Leod and Nita Clarke found organizations that had successful employee engagement programs see a significant increase in operating income:

▸ Companies with a highly engaged workforce experience a 19.2% growth in operating income over a 12-month period.

The Corporate Leadership Council studied the engagement level of 50,000 employees around the world to determine its direct impact on both employee performance and retention. Here are two important findings:

▸ Engaged companies grow profits as much as three times faster than their competitors do.

▸ Highly engaged employees are 87% less likely to leave the organization, resulting in significantly reduced turnover costs, hiring costs, onboarding costs, and training costs.

▸ The companies report twice as many customers who are loyal and engaged with the company.

▸ Companies reports twice the level of productivity.

▸ Companies have as much as a two-times lower turnover, resulting in a reduction in hiring and training expenses.

The results speak for themselves: If you want to grow, if you want to dominate your marketplace, than you need to fully engage your workforce.

While bottom-line results are important, those are really only part of what you gain from employee engagement. When you fully engage your team, you experience less workplace stress, more creativity and out-of-the box thinking, less drama, and a range of other powerful results that are difficult to measure.

By getting everyone fully involved, you increase the productivity of the team while decreasing the pressures on the individual. According to a study done by the Center for Creative Leadership, more than 80% of today's leaders report that their jobs are the primary reason for their level of stress. The pressure to produce results, win new customers, motivate your team, and grow the business is the responsibility of a leader. And without an engaged team, all of that responsibility is on the back of that leader. No wonder leaders are stressed.

As we discussed in the last chapter, engaging your team results in sharing the load, creating a joint venture, and making sure that everyone has a say and takes ownership in growing the business. With results like this, can you find one reason not to stop what you are doing and run—not walk—to begin fully engaging your team?

Employee engagement is often described as "discretionary effort." This is effort that is above and beyond the job description, which leads to innovation and increased creativity.

Interestingly enough, when employees are engaged, they work harder, are less entitled, and create a ground swell of new ideas. There is actually a domino effect among the team and their peers. The Gallup group discovered that more than 60% of engaged employees "feed" off the creativity of their peers, and almost that same percentage say their jobs drive their creativity to the strongest degree.

This is a chain of events that has benefits for everyone involved— employees, leadership, and customers. Bottom-line results are only part of the story; the true benefit comes in the form of behavioral returns, and that is where you receive the greatest return on investment. A more engaged team is one that is more driven to innovate, and a more innovative team is one that is far better positioned to succeed in today's changing environment.

## THE PROCESS OF INNOVATION

When it comes to the process of innovation, one of my favorite stories is about Amazon and the creation of Amazon Prime, arguably one of the most successful loyalty programs any company has ever created. It was actually a software engineer at Amazon who came up with the idea, after much time and energy was spent on figuring out the right loyalty program at the retailer. Note that this innovation, arguably one of the most important and successful programs Amazon has ever put into place, did not come from leadership—it was created with an engaged employee looking to make the company more successful, and the customer experience better.

The process of innovation includes a whole innovation life cycle, from idea creation to operational development and execution—then translation of those ideas into a new business, service level, or product within your company. One of the biggest factors in execution is the level to which the employee is engaged. People support, or are more likely to support, what they help create. An employee who helped design the new service or whose idea sparked the new product, is an employee who is passionate about ensuring that it is fully executed.

We have all been there, as leaders, on the other end of an employee who was unenthusiastic about your company, products, and services. Get that employee engaged, and not only you will get amazing, innovative ideas, but you will get an employee who is committed to the success of your organization.

## INSPIRING INNOVATION

So how does innovation happen, and how does it work? A great analogy is the one of the "dancing guy." In this concept, one lone man at a music festival stands apart and dances. Some observers laugh, some ignore him, and others watch. Then, someone else stands nearby and also dances. Soon, a few more join in, and in a short time it is an outright dance party.

In other words, the innovation was started by one, recognized by another who thought it was a good idea, and then others joined in; this enticed more to buy into the innovation, and then the majority quickly followed suit.

Is employee innovation like this? In many instances, yes. First, you have the culture in which one person has the courage to try something new, to innovate. That person "experiments" with a new process, product, method of improving customer relations, and so on. The key is creating a safe culture, where someone feels comfortable expressing an idea or trying something different, comfortable enough to come up with an innovative idea. From there, they enlist the support of another, who also sees something in the innovation, and together they influence the rest.

For innovation to truly work leadership is needed, someone who serves as a "champion." This is the person who assumes responsibility for forwarding or growing the innovative concept, and ensures it makes it past obstacles and challenges. The champion will walk it through whatever steps are required to ensure that it is a sound idea, and then take it to the next level.

For innovation to become more than a concept, it has to be a joint venture. Employees must feel safe enough to be creative and think outside the box. They need to feel assured that their opinions and ideas matter. Leadership needs to be supportive and committed to ensuring they first listen, then take action, and throw their muscle behind the idea to help it make it through the ranks.

## THE REAL WORLD

*At Studio Four Design, an architecture firm in Knoxville, Tennessee, innovation is far more than an idea or a leadership strategy—it is a way of life, engrained in their culture. Employees at every level of the organization, no matter their tenure or experience, describe themselves as problem-solvers, process-challengers, and see it is a major part of their job description to be constantly looking for new ways of doing things, challenging the status quo, and delivering exceptional work. Rather than waiting for leadership to tell them how to "do it better," they see it as their role to beat leadership to the punch.*

*Team members in and out of staff meetings question ideas, provide feedback (without being asked), and feel confident in the acceptance of their ideas and opinions. The results have ranged from creating operational efficiencies, to making new processes and systems, to staying on a job until it exceeds client expectations.*

*Innovation is not something that you can dictate, not something that you can force; it is motivated by the culture you create, and is key to the ownership, engagement, and overall success of your organization.*

## THE VALUE OF INNOVATION:

Innovation is a key initiative that ensures everyone wins, the benefits are global, and produce long-lasting results.

- ▸ The customer not only receives exceptional, high-quality products, but they are delivered via a highly engaged employee who cares.
- ▸ Employees feel heard, challenged to use their skills and talents, and, most importantly, connected to the success of the organization.
- ▸ Leaders are less stressed, as the responsibility of new ideas, increased service, and business growth is no longer just their job, but rather a joint venture between employee and leader.
- ▸ Bottom-line results and goals not only are easier to reach, but yield higher returns.
- ▸ Your atmosphere and workplace become a fun, productive, and enjoyable place to be.

The benefits—or Return On Investment (ROI)—of a culture supportive of employee innovation also include the rewards that employees gain. Your engagement programs may have already created some sort of recognition or reward systems, but they pale in comparison to the deeper rewards employees gain from the seeing their ideas or concepts brought to life.

## CREATING A SAFE CULTURE

However, as Bob Kelleher writes, some "leaders fail to create a safe environment for employees to contribute ideas. Worse, they create an environment in which new ideas are met with rejection."

It is easy enough to understand the "knee-jerk" reactions that leadership may have towards change. After all, we often hear, "If it isn't broken, why fix it?" That mindset, though, is what may be leading to the current state of affairs with employee engagement in general.

If you are to enjoy the many benefits and potential returns of employee innovation, you must create a culture that nurtures it in the first place. Create then protect your culture at all costs. Remember, culture is the engine of engagement and innovation.

Just consider what Forbes had to say about innovation: "Over the past several years, business articles and research studies have stressed significance in creating long-lasting competitive advantage and achieving dramatic increases in organizational performance. The source of these things is innovation."

More than 700 CEOs surveyed by IBM Consulting Services pointed to innovation as one of the primary mechanisms behind their growth, and cited new ideas in business models, as well as in services, products, and markets as the areas where innovation occurred.

Innovation does not happen in a vacuum, and it is rare that the isolated worker has an "Ah ha!" moment. Instead, the company cultures that develop community, encourage work in groups, and create opportunities for employees to think freely or brainstorm have the greatest track records of innovation.

As Gallup's most recent employee engagement research indicates, "Engaged employees are far more likely to suggest or develop creative ways to improve management or business processes. They're also far more likely to find creative ways to solve customer problems or to involve their customers in creating service innovations."

That is a perfect illustration of the proverbial "win-win" scenario, but in this case, there is a bonus—a third "win" that gets added to the equation. When a safe culture is created, leadership and employees are engaged, innovation happens, and the customers also win. Your organization becomes a triple threat, creating the best environment for customers, employees, and leadership.

As Gallup concluded, "Company leaders who want to drive growth through innovation should first create an environment that not only welcomes new ideas but almost expects them, and should make engaging employees a key component of that strategy."

You have already integrated engagement into your business strategy, but now you have an even greater incentive to do so. You now know that growth and innovation are natural outcomes, too.

## WELLBEING IS PART OF THE ROI

When you actively create an environment that welcomes employee innovation (as a natural byproduct of your employee engagement efforts), the return on your investment is substantial.

Your "investment" can mean many things, depending upon your current company or organization's status. While there may be the obvious financial investments needed to implement some aspects of your programs, you are also investing the time and effort to initiate the programs, changes, and follow-up required.

It is not unusual to hear leadership and managers admit to struggling with the issue of new engagement programs. In fact, it is such a common dilemma that Gallup published a report on strategies for making programs "stick."

In it, they noted that "businesses seek the benefits that come from increased engagement—improved productivity, profitability, safety, retention, and customer focus, among others—but they don't feel that employee engagement is becoming integrated into the company's culture."

This means it is something that is discussed and created at the surface but never introduced into the inner workings of the company, never implemented as a true part of the culture. Luckily for you, your newfound knowledge and plans for employee engagement will help create the culture ideally suited to long-term engagement and innovation.

And while you will see remarkable improvements in productivity, profits, retention, customer loyalty, and whatever other goals you set for your programs, there is one more hidden benefit of engagement that is often overlooked. We overlook it because it is hard to measure: the wellbeing of your team.

Making space for innovation is a way of enabling your employees to take advantage of the engagement "outlets." Whether this is a series of ongoing meetings, a specific local level leader, or another channel, engagement opens communication and makes it safe to address many issues. It also sets the stage for sharing ideas and inspiring innovation.

However, a report on employee-driven innovation has this to say about it:

Participation of both skilled and unskilled staff members have a supportive and stimulating effect. Although financial measures are the primary evaluation base for most companies to implement employee engagement programs. Other soft effects include reduced stress, lower absence rates, greater job satisfaction, happy employees and thus a higher retention rate.

Wellbeing, then, is another hidden benefit. Employee engagement programs have benefits that go far beyond the bottom line, setting the stage for tremendous growth and clear competitive advantage.

## IN THEIR OWN WORDS...

"The best measure of employee engagement is the level of 'inventiveness' that people demonstrate in their daily work. By engaging the heart and creating a deep sense of personal accountability for the success of the team or organization, you engage the most vital part of a person's conviction to get things done. By engaging the mind, you ignite their most creative thinking, as they devise solutions that may never have occurred to you or them. The power of gaining people's hearts and minds in getting things done may seem obvious, but the price you pay when they only apply their hands and feet to a task, while not so obvious, is nonetheless real. People who invest their hearts and minds take accountability and go beyond the basic requirements of their jobs and work to make things happen in a way that may even surpass your wildest expectations."

- Partners in Leadership

## CALL TO ACTION

1. *Define Innovation - Establish with leadership that this is a desired result of creating an employee engagement program.*

2. *Create A Culture – Make a culture where ideas are encouraged, nurtured, and developed. Design opportunities for associates to work together, think outside the box, and brainstorm.*

3. *Make Your Culture Safe - Make a "safe" place to express ideas, to challenge the status quo, and even to fail. Reward the idea as often or more often than you do the result.*

4. *Protect Your Culture - At all costs, make sure that leaders understand you value innovation, and that team members realize this is something that leadership wants.*

5. *Ask yourself and hold yourself accountable to the following questions:*

   *What are you doing to ensure that innovation is nurtured in your workforce?*

   *What are you doing to show you "value" innovation?*

   *What opportunities are you creating (project teams, brainstorming, etc.) to inspire innovation?*

## PART I CONCLUDING THOUGHTS

You have completed the first part of this critical journey to create a culture of employee engagement that inspires, motivates, and delivers ownership at every level. At this point, you should realize that employee engagement is transformational for your organization, your leaders, your customers, and your employees. Employee engagement is one of those rare business strategies that have a powerful, positive impact on everyone they touch.

Now let's move on to how you transform leaders, employees, or both; these next two sections are going to show you how to step up to the plate, take ownership, and get results, no matter your role in the company.

# PART II

## LEADERSHIP - CREATING A CULTURE OF INNOVATION

You have heard the saying "Change starts at the top." I'm not sure that has ever been more true than in this economy. With your newfound knowledge from Part I, you get it: As the leader, the change has got to start with you! This is a new economy, one that has drastically changed your customers and employees, and one that calls for all hands on deck, with everyone fully engaged if you are going to succeed.

Though you can find scores of resources promising to "get your employees engaged," you need to remember that as a leader, you can create the environment, but whether or not an employee engages is up to him. The act of engagement is emotional, so the will to work has to come from within. You, as the leader, can create the culture, but it is the employee who chooses to (or not to) engage.

As the leader, you are still in charge, you still get to determine, direct, and shape the vision for the organization, but the goals you set or ideas you give cannot be shaped as directives, policy, or command. Instead, your leadership style needs to shift from tell-direct to inclusive, so you can create a culture where everyone understands how to own that role. Create a culture that at all times encourages employees to strive to do their part in driving growth and success, and reaching established goals.

The term "everyone" includes the highest levels of leadership, as well as the frontline. Truly immersing employees in the process of engagement is something every leader of the organization must exhibit if the program has any chance of real success.

In the first part of this book, you uncovered some basic concepts and strategies to put to work in your "paradigm shift." You discovered that you may need to completely redesign how you solicit employee feedback, design surveys, take action on the employee input, and communicate effectively. You learned that ownership is both a strategy to engage and a benefit from a strong employee engagement program, one that results in innovation that even further engages employees and spurs the growth and transformation of the company.

Up until now, our discussions have been more theoretical and general. Why? Because in order to really implement a new type of employee engagement program, you need to understand why it is important, and the impact it has on the employee, the overall team, your customers, and bottom-line results. Most  importantly, you need to understand what is in it for you, as the leader, and hopefully by now you realize and understand there is quite a bit to gain.

By now you should be ready to go, champing at the bit to get started. Well, the plan now is to simplify the process. Sure, you are smart, and you can figure it out, but in this part of the book we are going to give you the specific steps, strategies, and actions you need to fully implement a strong employee engagement program. This part of the book is where we are going to take what we have learned about employees' perspectives in order to "tap into" their motivation and help them engage fully.

As you might perceive from the first part, it takes a new sort of leadership perspective to do this. Before you can transform your team, you yourself need to transform, going from a leader who wants to be in charge to one who wants to serve.

In the current climate, you will have a new role. It is one in which you will reshape the culture of the company, building an environment in which those employees who want to tap into their motivation, actively accept personal responsibility, and fully engage in innovation easily can do so.

In other words, in this part we learn how to move from your former role as the heroic leader with the weight of success or failure entirely on your shoulders, to the transformational leader who is both able and eager to take action and help employees to engage at the deepest levels possible.

## IN THEIR OWN WORDS...

"Over 40 years ago, a German psychologist grew interested in how humans learn. He ran an experiment where he taught a six-step process to transfer water between two containers. After the explanation, he had people practice this technique a few times. He then demonstrated a 3-step process to transfer the water. Despite the obvious ease of the new and improved method, only fifty percent of the group used it. Luchen's realized that humans quickly form habits. Unfortunately, once a habit forms it's difficult to modify, even when the new behavior is clearly better than the old... Habits also form in organizations.

Organizational dry rot takes many forms. A particularly insidious form consists of a state of complacency were individuals believe, 'It ain't broke,' and 'It doesn't need fixing.' This love of the status quo is especially dangerous... To survive, organizations must grow and adapt. They must continually try out and adapt new ideas. And that is why they need transformational leaders."

- Murray Johannsen

# CHAPTER 10

## THE POWER OF LEADERSHIP

t is hard to believe, but one person, one individual, really can start that journey that ultimately transforms a company and reinvents an industry. And if change is really going to happen in your company and your industry, that person needs to be you.

In today's economy, so many professions are struggling beyond economics, they are struggling to find talent, to keep talent, and to understand how this new economy is impacting their industry and their clients.

Leaders in professions like banking, law, insurance, and accounting are just a few that are facing the challenge of attracting and retaining key employees and top talent. According to an article in Bloomberg, law school applications are at a fifteen-year low, and according to a report produced by Digital Intelligence Systems, LLC (DISYS), the financial services industry not only struggles to find top talent but "lives in fear" that their top talent will leave. The list of industries and organizations facing these challenges is endless.

As we have discussed in previous chapters, today's talent wants more and is looking for something different when it comes to an organization and profession to commit themselves to for a job, let alone a career. That "something different" is dependent upon leadership, and in order to transform our organizations and industries, we need to start by transforming leadership.

THE REAL WORLD

## ONE LEADER INSPIRES A MOVEMENT

*HORNE LLP is a top-50 accounting firm that, through visionary leadership and a strong commitment to people, is transforming not only their firm, but the entire accounting profession. HORNE has declared an official War on Accounting Firm Culture, and has asked others to join in the transformation. Beginning with a clearly articulated vision and the courage of the partner group to commit to building an amazing culture, the entire organization is now committed to building the Wise Firm© and becoming the firm of the future.*

*In 2011, Joey Havens presented the vision of the Wise Firm© to the partners of HORNE. Passionately and persuasively, he told a story of the urgent need to change, to transform how they work and how they lead, facing head-on the challenges and the changes facing this profession.*

*Considered by some to be a radical approach, the Wise Firm©, shared by Joey Havens and embraced throughout the firm, is the name given to this cultural transformation at HORNE. A constant work in progress, a "journey," as they refer to it at HORNE, it is how they describe both who they are, and who they are aspiring to be. Based on the Biblical parable of a wise man who built his house on a strong foundation and who weathered great storms, the Wise Firm© is the clearly defined plan, the roadmap that outlines the specific building blocks required to create the great culture they have envisioned. For more about Horne and the Wise Firm©, click through to this link: http://www.meridithelliottpowell. com/?s=The+WISE+FIRM&post_type=post*

*Leadership is a powerful force and is the catalyst needed to create a culture of employee engagement, one that inspires ownership at every level and innovation at every turn.*

*Merriam-Webster says that transformation is "a complete or major change," and that is what is needed in the field of leadership if you are going to move from an organization that requires engagement to one that inspires it. And as we know, inspiration is the only true way to create a fully engaged team.*

*Somewhere along the way, leadership became an expected next step on the corporate ladder, rather than something that requires a certain set of skills, has high expectations, and comes with a proven track record of developing people. In interviews of leaders in the field of education and human resources for a White Paper on Employee Engagement, more than half said that one of their major issues related to employee engagement was leadership and their lack of understanding of how to lead. They went on to share that the problem was created because of the lack of horizontal promotional opportunities within their organizations. That challenge had created too many leaders who were promoted for their performance, not for their ability (or desire) to lead, develop, and truly engage people.*

*When we look at transforming leadership, that is where we need to begin. W eneed to not only transform the current leaders we have, but we need to transform how we choose leaders and what we require of them. To understand how to transform leadership, let's take a look at how we define leadership.*

## LEADERSHIP MODELS – HOW THEY DIFFER

In 1978, author James MacGregor Burns won the Pulitzer Prize for his publication entitled, simply, Leadership. In it, he broke apart the many kinds of leadership throughout history and described one as "transforming." This was a form immediately embraced by many, as it engaged the "full person" (both of the leader and follower) and led to a symbiotic benefit in which both parties stimulated one another towards success.

He also described a form of leadership known as "heroic." This type creates a relationship between a follower and leader in which tremendous faith is placed in the leader's skills in tackling crises or obstacles.

It is relatively easy to see how heroic leadership is flawed. In heroic leadership all of the power and ownership is placed into the hands of the leader. Though it can be argued that "one would be hard pressed to find a situation in which followers lacked confidence in their leader and a favorable outcome ensued," the point is that this approach is out of balance (Cohen, 2010).

The challenge of heroic leaders is calling all the shots; while that sounds great on the surface, there are far more challenges than benefits to being a heroic leader. When you make all the decisions, you get little outside investment and support, and all of the blame if and when things do not work. Heroic leaders also have to be the sole muscle for their idea, pushing the team to do what it takes to make the idea a success. So yes, while heroic leadership sounds great from the outside, when you look behind the scenes, it is arguably one of the major reasons your team is not engaging.

When a leader leads in the heroic style there is no substantial role, no role with purpose, for the employee. Without purpose and without clarity of role, you never tap into the employee's intrinsic drive and internal motivation, and thus no real engagement ever happens. This means that with traditional leadership styles, leaders are working harder and employees are working less. That model is not only outdated, but also dangerous in a time when competition is high, consumers are demanding, and margins are tighter than ever.

It is time for a new type of leader, one who understands the shift and is ready to lead in the new economy.

## THE TRANSFORMATIVE LEADER

Now, we do not want to cast heroic leadership in a totally bad light, or make you think that there is not a time and a place for it, because there is. There are multiple styles of leadership, and certain times call for certain styles. Hero leaders can be thought of as leaders who are needed during times of "war," whether on the battlefield or in the competitive landscape. When the bottom is falling out, the competitive threat is getting powerful, or the ship is sinking, I would argue you need someone in charge—telling everyone what to do, keeping them accountable, and firing those who do not comply.

But while wartime hero leaders are important, they are not the right type of leader when you are building, expanding, creating culture, and engaging employees. When you want ownership and innovation at every level, when you want the best from your people, and ideas from the bottom up, you need a growth leader—you need a transformational leader.

Hero leadership worked when you could promise your teams long-term employment, a pension, and the faith that they would not be downsized or their jobs moved to India. But you cannot promise that anymore, even if you wanted to, because no one knows what the future holds.

Gone are the days when employees were willing to give up a little say in their futures or more impact on their jobs in exchange for steady paycheck and the security of a job. With those things off the table, employees want more, and they require it in exchange for innovative ideas and loyalty.

So again, new times call for new leadership.

Transformational leaders intimately get to know their teams, interact with others, create working relationships that are more like joint ventures. They build environments that foster community, connection, and trust.

As one expert wrote, "Leaders transform their followers through their inspirational nature and charismatic personalities. Rules and regulations are flexible, guided by group norms. These attributes provide a sense of belonging for the followers as they can easily identify with the leader and its purpose."

Clearly, if any statement can better describe how this is the age for transformational leadership, it would be hard to find it.

## ARE YOU TRANSFORMATIONAL?

You have done some outward and inward assessments on an organizational level. You know about your options and resources, you may have identified some weaknesses in your engagement programs, and you may already be formulating some solid plans for transforming your workplace into one that is prime for complete employee engagement.

The next thing to determine, though, is if your approach to leadership (even with your new understanding of all of the issues relating to employee engagement) is actually transformational. It is far easier to understand transformational leadership than it is to practice it. Even if it is something you desire and strive for, all too often, when we move into leadership positions ourselves, we revert to the leadership styles we know and understand, ones that were modeled for us. More often than not, that is the style of heroic leadership.

Psychology Today offers a very clear explanation of transformational

## IN THEIR OWN WORDS...

### THE TRANSFORMATIONAL LEADERSHIP STYLE

Transformational leadership is about implementing new ideas; these individuals continually change themselves; they stay flexible and adaptable; and continually improve those around them. Transformational leaders has been written about for thousands of years

http://www.legacee.com/Info/Leadership/LeaderResourcesTop.html

- Legacee.com

leadership, saying, "Transformational leaders focus on followers, motivating them to high levels of performance, and in the process, help followers develop their own leadership potential."

## THE REAL WORLD

*Stacy Cox and his partners, Michael Keller, Greg Terry, and Kevin Diegel, all set out to be transformational leaders. That was the goal, without ever hearing the word or understanding the concept.*

*Studio Four Design's founding partners came together over a number of years after working together in other larger firms with cultures that were manager-driven and not leader-driven. The cultures they came from did not express or practice the values they wanted in a firm, let alone the way they wanted team members and employees to work and relate to one another.*

*With no formal leadership training and no great role models, they set out to start a firm that was "different." Intrinsically, they knew there had to be something better. But as happens all too often, the workload, the demands of running a company, and the very fact that they were successful quickly, created the excuse not to "rock the boat."*

*So instead of becoming the truly transformational firm they wanted to be, they settled for creating a better place to work than where they had come from, implementing programs like transparency, an open work environment, and team rewards and recognition.*

*It was not until the economic bubble hit in 2008 that the wakeup call came and things started to shift. True to their values, they were servant leaders, making sure that their employees got paychecks when at times they themselves did not. Despite the justification to do it, they chose not to lay off anyone at that time, and kept work coming in and expenses down.*

*While they were killing themselves, it seemed that some of their employees did not care, and they realized they were far from being the company that they had envisioned Studio Four Design to be. This was just the gift they needed. They realized that becoming the leaders and the company they wanted to be would mean more than just finding more work and more employees. They knew that they needed to embrace and understand what real leadership was and hone their skills to practice it. They started a journey together to commit to a process of learning what it took to become the leaders they needed to be. The leaders that could create the company that they wanted Studio Four Design to be.*

This journey has had amazing impact on their company in terms of creating a culture of the best and brightest, with a healthy pipeline of clients, innovation and ideas coming from every direction, strong growth, and a fully engaged team. But the biggest lesson they have learned is that this journey is never over, it never ends; as a team, they need to continue to grow, learn, and implement. For transformational leaders, the leadership skill set is in a constant state of change and growth, and only those leaders who are committed to personal and organizational growth will continue to transform their organizations.

So how do you know if you are a transformational leader, or if you are still modeling the leadership style of the past? It may help you to look at the four I's of true transformational leadership. In doing so, you can better gauge where you are on the journey to becoming transformational:

▸ Idealized Influence - Are you a role model who is always "walking the walk" rather than preaching company goals or policies?

▸ Inspirational Motivation - Transformational leaders inspire, and they motivate others to follow.

▸ Individualized Consideration - It is easy enough to say that you care about employees, but the transformational leader has genuine concern for the feelings and needs of her employees, giving them personal attention both in business and in life.

▸ Intellectual Stimulation - Challenging her teams to do their best, the transformational leader actually pushes her teams to be creative, innovative, and grow. She leads through the power of the question.

A transformational leader understands that her path to success is through the full engagement of her employees Focusing on employees, demonstrating care, and providing them with the tools they need to thrive, prosper, and grow are essential.

Keep in mind that we have looked at leadership in terms of "foundation building" and the creation of a "framework." This too is part of transformational leadership, as it creates the setting in which employees can engage and enjoy the maximum benefits of your leadership.

Of course, the relationship is rewarding for all involved, and there are major returns on your investments in first assessing your leadership, shifting to the transformational model, and laying that framework.

Owning your role as a leader means accepting the responsibility for creating the kind of atmosphere needed for optimal employee engagement. As Murray Johannsen writes, transformational leaders are "not creatures of the status quo." They are not only about change; they are intuitive about it, tending to be among the most emotionally intelligent people too.

Though there are many ways emotional intelligence is viewed and described, let's just take it at its most basic level—emotionally intelligent people are those who can read others' emotions as well as their own. To become a transformational leaders you need to develop your emotional intelligence so you can better connect with and tap into the emotional engagement of your employees.

## IN THEIR OWN WORDS...

"The transforming approach clearly has much to recommend it. These include significant positive change in people and organizations, changes in perceptions and values, and changes in the expectations and aspirations of those led. Most importantly, it is different from transactional leadership in that it is not based on an exchange relationship, but on the leader's personality, traits and ability to create change through example and articulation of a vision, goals, and tasks. Transforming leaders are idealized because they are not focused on benefits to self, but on benefits for the organization, its members, and those they serve."

(Burns, 1978)

## CALL TO ACTION

1. *Determine Your Leadership Style – Let's determine your leadership style and your leadership culture! Be honest; take some time to think about where and when you are transformational, and then where and when you are heroic. Then work the process to move the needle to transformational.*

2. *A great way to start is by assessing your leadership based on the Four I's, and by posing the following questions, taken directly from a psychological test designed to measure transformational leadership skills. Answer these statements with a "yes" or "no":*

   ▸ *I would never require a follower to do something that I wouldn't do myself.*

   ▸ *My followers would say that they know what I stand for.*

   ▸ *Inspiring others has always come easy to me.*

   ▸ *My followers have told me that my enthusiasm and positive energy are infectious.*

   ▸ *My followers would say that I am very attentive to their needs and concerns.*

   ▸ *Even though I could easily do a task myself, I delegate it to expand my followers' skills.*

   ▸ *Team creativity and innovation are the keys to success.*

   ▸ *I encourage my followers to question their most basic way of thinking.*

3. *Assess your answers and for that you are "no" responses, understand you are still using the older models. Start to build your plans for transforming your leadership approach into the*

*transformational model by considering the ways you might convert any negative answers into resounding positives.*

*As the leader, you have taken ownership of your role. That is a transformational role that is willing to take risks, make changes when data reveals it to be required, and begin engaging your modern employees in the best ways possible.*

# CHAPTER 11

## SETTING THE TONE

One of the major differences between a heroic leader and a transformational leader is focus. The heroic leader focuses on goals and results; the transformational leader focuses on people and talent development. Both are looking to grow the organization, and both want to increase profits and build the bottom line, they just see and experience the path to get there very differently. As a leader, where and how you focus makes all the difference.

Transformational leaders believe (and act on the belief) that the path to profitability is through the engagement level of their employees. They believe the more talented, passionate, and engaged their team, the more successful they will be. Leaders affect their employees in many important ways, the three most significant being:

▶ Setting the tone

▶ Creating the right atmosphere

▶ Building the culture

How you influences your team in these three areas will dictate the type of change you create and the kind of employee you engage.

As the Cornell HR Review said, "Employees rely on their manager or leader to model the behaviors expected of them and give them the space to grow and develop. The transformational leadership style allows for exactly this."

## SET THE TONE

If we look back at the Four I's of transformational leadership qualities, recall that there are the II (Idealized Influence) and the IM (Inspirational Motivation). These attributes are desirable in leadership, in general, because they allow employees to feel that they are "working under a visible and inspired leadership team that promotes and role models honesty, integrity, respect, collaboration, and trust" (Tuuk, 2012).

In other words, leadership sets the tone for all other employees with their words, their communication, but, in reality, the alignment of that tone with their actions and values truly communicates to the employees who they are and what the organization stands for.

It is always easy enough to say, this is what we are without having to take the actions to "show" what you are. However, when your transformational leadership is built on the framework of "setting the tone," it has to live up to the established ideals (i.e. a mission statement, values) that are meant to inspire if you ever hope to truly engage your employees.

Remember, just like today's consumers, employees are highly skeptical, well informed, and squarely in control. If you do not practice what you preach, if you are not careful to align what you say with what you do, your employees will know it and will model back to you the behavior you have modeled to them. That is kind of scary, isn't it? As a transformational leader, I want you to see these as unit, tone, actions, values, a unit that needs to be seamless, transparent and aligned. Meaning you need to know your values,

Setting tone is about establishing the culture: the vision of it,

## IN THEIR OWN WORDS...

"According to James McGregor Burns, Transformational Leadership is when 'leaders and their followers raise one another to higher levels of morality and motivation.' ... You need to think about whether you want to make progress because of where your name appears on an org chart, or because people buy into your vision. Early on in my career, I wanted to make a difference because I saw the status quo was not getting the job done. I was pretty low on the org chart so I had to find other ways to get others engaged. It turns out, other people want to see change occur as well. They may be overwhelmed with where to start, or think that their efforts would be wasted. But a small group of people can rally together to influence change as seen many times in history. Using Transformational Leadership may sound like another buzz phrase but in reality, it's a few easy changes."

- Doyle, 2015

the mission of how it is to be carried out, and the goals needed to ensure it happens. Tone is about answering the questions of "what" the organization or team needs to accomplish. To set the tone, a transformational leader relies on well-developedthe guiding principles and standards that the team can use as a touchstone. This touchstone helps to hold you accountable and to ensure you and your team remain focused on a common vision.

Tone creates a common language, a common understanding, which is as easy for a new employee to understand as it is for a long-time employee to embrace. Tone ensures everyone from executive leadership to front-line personnel is sure about the direction the company is headed, and their role in helping the organization get there.

Again, tone is a small, but significant piece of the puzzle, and to truly move into the role of a transformational leader, you need to follow tone with the right atmosphere.

## CREATE THE ATMOSPHERE

I like to think of tone as saying what you want to accomplish; atmosphere is creating what you want the culture to feel like, the experience you want the employees and team to have when they are working there. Atmosphere is hard to wrap your head around, but it is powerful. Most of us spend far more time at work and with our team members than we do with our own families, so if you want employees to engage, it needs to be a place where people want to work.

## THE BIG AH-HA!

I interviewed a number of CEOs, leaders, and individuals for this book, and in doing my research, one thing stood out as the biggest consistency I observed: Organizations with an engaged team had employees who genuinely liked each other, enjoyed working together, and had a sense of community.

No matter the industry, as I met with teams, walked through buildings, and observed meetings, I found people who worked hard (and produced a lot), laughed, joked, and genuinely enjoyed each other's company. The atmosphere in every single one of these organizations communicated that this was a place these individuals truly enjoyed being.

So how do you create atmosphere? First, you have to establish what it is you want the atmosphere to be, look like, and feel like. This is not just some place you want to work, but some place the best and brightest would want to work.

To set the right atmosphere, you need to ask the right people, those leaders and those employees you truly enjoy working there, and those you want to or are engaged. Begin by asking them what they want the work environment to look and feel like. If your culture is to be an enjoyable place to work, and a place where your vision and your mission is to be accomplished, what do they need from you in order to create that atmosphere.

Creating the right atmosphere is about developing an environment that reflects your values and aligns with your vision and mission. It is about creating a place where the type of employees you want, are the type of employees you attract.

Once it is established, you need to ensure that leadership incentivizes the behaviors that reinforce and support your atmosphere. To engage, employees need a say in what they want their work environment to look and feel like, but to make it happen, leaders need to ensure they formally and informally reward those behaviors.

## THE REAL WORLD

*Studio Four Design has created a fun yet powerful rewards program that ensures their team understands they are serious about their corporate atmosphere.*

*Having worked hard to create and implement their core values, and having come from places where the values were nothing but words on a sheet of paper, the leadership team of Studio Four Design wanted to ensure they built a different environment.*

*So after a process of discovery about who they are and why they do what they do, they developed their core values. To reinforce them and their desired behaviors, they created CORE VALUES awards, a reward and recognition program that focuses solely on honoring those team members who most exhibit the company's values: Go Beyond; Invest in Yourself; Value Others; and Empower & Collaborate.*

*Individual core value awards are given mid-year with the annual Blue Vase Award (given to the employee who exhibits the strongest example of all four core values), given at the company Christmas party. While this program is unique and fun (the trophies that go with this award are unusual to say the least—vintage trophies purchased on eBay that make you laugh just to look at them), it is the pride these employees take in them that helps you understand their purpose in creating an engaging atmosphere.*

*Proudly displayed on top of employee desks within clear view of team members and clients alike, it is easy to see that at Studio Four Design it is as important to be good at what you do, as it is to Go Beyond, Invest In Yourself, Value Others, and Empower & Collaborate.*

*Your firm has a vision, and you have developed the values and goals to ensure achieving that vision. You set the tone by living up to that vision, by creating an atmosphere in which all employees are supported, rewarded, and encouraged when they exhibit the values and behaviors that make the atmosphere a place where you actually want to be.*

## BUILD THE CULTURE

*Tone and atmosphere lead to culture, and the right culture leads to innovation, ownership, and a fully engaged team.*

Consider what Jon Katzenbach has to say on the matter:

Leaders may try to ignore their culture and act as if it isn't important. But when overlooked, the hidden power of a company's culture can thwart any leader's strategic aspirations. No matter how many top-down directives you issue, they will rarely be executed. Cultures can be diagnosed best by the work behaviors they promote. Do people collaborate easily? Do they make decisions individually or in groups? Are they open with their information? Do they reflect on successes and failures and learn from them?

Another CEO, Tony Hsieh of Zappos.com, says that culture is the key:

"If you get the culture right, most of the other stuff will just take care of itself." And though this is an oversimplification, as creating culture takes work to create and even more work to sustain, the point is spot on.

So what is company culture, how does it differ from tone and atmosphere, and how does a transformational leader create the right culture?

## THE REAL WORLD

*When HORNE Executive Partner Joey Havens shared the Wise Firm© vision, the name of their company culture, he helped develop descriptive, distinct building blocks of the Wise Firm©. Together, the overall Wise Firm© vision and specific building blocks work to articulate both who they are and who they aspire to be.*

*That descriptive vision is important, because transformational leaders understand that you never "finish" transforming. The building blocks of the Wise Firm© are the roadmap, the blueprint, to building a culture that the engaged team of HORNE are embracing, owning, growing, and making stronger.*

## CALL TO ACTION

1. *Heroic vs. Transformational - Ensure you understand the difference between a heroic leader and a transformational leader.*

2. *Establish which one you are (chances are you are a combination of both), and determine the skills, habits, and behaviors you need to change to become a transformational leader.*

3. *Create a Transformational Leadership Strategy:*

   ▶ *Set the tone.*

   ▶ *Develop the atmosphere.*

   ▶ *Create the culture.*

   ▶ *Begin with engaging the team in the process to ensure you develop a company that reflects an organization that looks and feels comfortable not only to you, but also to those types of employees you want to attract and retain.*

4. *Reward & Recognize*

   ▶ *Ensure not only that employees understand the culture, but that they are rewarded and recognized when they work in a way that invigorates and moves that culture forward.*

# CHAPTER 12

## SPARK EMPLOYEE INNOVATION

have had a lot of less-than-desirable jobs in my day, including but not limited to: dishwasher, waitress, bus boy, and short order cook. But one I avoided, although was offered several times, was retail worker. Now, don't take this personally if you work retail and love it—it just has never been my cup of tea. I prefer waiting tables, which I am sure is distasteful (understandably) to many people. But I say that because I interviewed a young woman for this book who felt the exact same way I did about retail. Yet, despite the fact that it was the last job on earth she wanted to do, she was so disengaged with her leader and her organization that she quit her professional job, the job she had gone to school to learn to do, to work retail. At the time it was the only other job she could find, and while not something she wanted to do, it was, in her mind, more engaging than where she was.

That is the power of a culture of engagement. She is back working in her profession now, and thriving in her new company due to an engaging culture and a committed leadership team. It is easy to see the dynamo her first employer missed, all because he had no idea how to spark, let alone create, a culture of employee engagement.

In short, employees have many options and are not often locked into sticking around in a job they feel is unsatisfactory. In most cases, they won't stick around. Today's employees (just like today's customers) have too many choices, and they don't hesitate to look elsewhere for a better "deal."

As a transformational leader, it is your job to let go of ego, to realize you are not in the power seat; and the best way to gain competitive advantage is to create a culture that not only attracts the best and brightest, but sparks their innovation.

Engagement is about creating the opportunity for employees to emotionally connect. Provide a culture that ensures they feel cared about, which in turn guarantees they care about their team, their company, and their customers. When an employee actively engages, the natural outcome is innovation, and innovation is where as a leader and a company your return on investment starts to pay dividends.

Not only have you created an atmosphere where the best and brightest want to work, but you have created an atmosphere where they care, where they are motivated, and where they want to contribute. They are anxious to share their ideas, their solutions, their strategies for growth and for enhancing the client experience, and all of that is innovation.

I have to admit, if you read this book and all you learned was to make a tiny step to improve your culture, I would be happy. No—I would be thrilled! But to get all this book has to offer, to really take your organization to the next level, you need to understand the value of innovation:

1. It is that "something," that deeper level of engagement that allows businesses to achieve far greater success then their competitors, with an ease and a flow that is almost counterintuitive. It takes less effort and yields better results.

2. It is that "something" that deepens motivation, turning it into passion and drive, and that seamlessly boosts retention rates with your highest employees and makes you a magnet for the best and the brightest.

3. It is what ensures ideas and solutions flow as strongly bottom-up as they do top-down, meaning everyone on your team—everyone—owns and feels responsible for the success of the organization.

Why would innovation boost retention? After all, when you create a culture of employee innovation, it is the employees, not you as the leader, who are working harder, putting in more effort, and freely sharing great ideas and intellectual capital. But interestingly enough (and it is what I love about this topic), it is the strategies used to inspire innovation (which we cover below) that make any workplace more likely to retain employees over the long term.

Consider what Inc. Magazine says: "No job is too simple or mundane for a boss to give employees room to innovate. While employees might be suspicious at first if they've never been presented with such decision making power before, they will often not just adapt to, but thrive in, an environment that gives them additional control."

Naturally, you cannot just order employees to innovate, nor can you wait around and hope that the work you have done will automatically bring innovation. While we wish it were that easy, there is some complexity in tapping into your employees' innovative spirits, and throughout the next few chapters we'll explore three strategies that you can use to awaken their innovation and allow it to lead your team and organization towards success.

The three strategies are:

1. Trust

2. Ownership

3. Performance

Note that I did not describe them as factors, issues, areas, or anything else. That is because they are strategic steps required to create change and transformation. Prior to instituting such strategies, though, you need to be clear about employee engagement, simply because it too is a major part of what drives innovation.

## ENGAGEMENT ALWAYS RELATES TO INNOVATION

In the previous chapter, we considered your role as a leader, and what you had to address in order to set the tone. The last point was your company culture, and, at that time, we noted that without culture, no tone or atmosphere could be created. Nor can there be innovation without it.

With that in mind, let's take a moment to really understand this: Engagement is related to emotion. It is the emotional attachment you feel to your job or organization that leads you to go beyond the expected, to make discretionary efforts that help the organization achieve then surpass their goals.

So, engagement comes from an emotional basis. Your culture also has that emotional component too. As one formal definition notes, "it is the values and behaviors that contribute to the unique social and psychological environment of that organization" (BusinessDictionary. com). Thus, experiences, expectations, values, philosophies, shared beliefs, customs, written and unwritten rules or norms, they are all part of the unique social and psychological environment.

Again, that is the importance of knowing and understanding the values and behaviors that you want and need to spark engagement and innovation, and then rewarding them. Because if at any time you are out of alignment, not walking your walk, do you know what happens? You shatter trust, or worse there is no culture for shared beliefs or expectations. You can easily see where this is going. That negative psychological impact triggers emotional responses from leaders and employees, and they grow disinterested, bored, weary, resentful. In other words, they disengage.

Recall that CEO Jon Katzenbach said, "Cultures can be diagnosed best by the work behaviors they promote. Do people collaborate easily? Do they make decisions individually or in groups? Are they open with their information? Do they reflect on successes and failures and learn from them? Do they ensure and commit to the goals and vision of the organization?"

Ideally, your culture answers those questions in the affirmative. Yet it is not easy to build this sort of culture. It does demand some major effort on the part of the transformational leadership, and it is not a "one-shot" effort but an ongoing one that needs to be supported, updated, and constantly reinforced.

Fortunately, those three strategies can help you to create something that is relatively self-sustaining,  and one that will not require a reinvention of the wheel on an ongoing basis. As a result, long-time and new employees will all exist in an atmosphere ripe for challenge, growth, and innovation.

Creativity and Motivation

When your team members understand and act on the understanding that your success, the company's success, and their individual success are one and the same, that is the day you have truly tapped their motivation and unlocked their creativity. That is the day that your employees have fully engaged.

So how do you get there? How, even as a transformational leader, do you not only communicate that message but confirm they understand and embrace it beyond surface? It all comes back to the three ideas that we will more fully explore in the coming chapters. As you can see, they tie directly to the three strategies (trust, ownership and performance) we will be exploring:

▸ Autonomy - Ensuring employees feel a measure of control (Trust)

▸ Competence - Allowing employees to succeed in what they are doing (Performance)

▸ Relatedness - Ensuring employees connect with others in the organization (Ownership)

Employee engagement and change have both been tagged as key strategies for a transformational leader. You will be able to begin doing so as you look at these three strategies necessary for innovation.

One story of employee innovation explains the issue nicely. It focuses on a group of garbage men in a planned community, whose "supervisor encouraged them to improve upon the existing methods for collecting garbage. One employee discovered a way to cut the route in half, saving both time and fuel costs. By carrying an empty can with him on his route, he only had to make one trip between the truck and each house instead of two." (Spiro, 2010)

The supervisor trusted his team with the chance to problem solve, while also challenging them—thereby letting them have ownership in their role and giving them a chance to innovate in a way that could be measured in terms of performance.

Innovation is really that simple; it just requires some steps that go beyond the simple illustration just given.

## CALL TO ACTION

1. *Ask Yourself:*

   *What is the current culture of my organization? Is it one that is ready for innovation, or do I have more work to do to set the stage?*

   *Is my team ready for a transfer of power, and a more shared style of leadership?*

2. *Prepare Your Team:*

   *You may laugh at that, but so often I have seen employees who say they want engagement, an opportunity to innovate, but when the time presents itself, they find they are too locked in their paradigm, too frozen in fear, and too used to doing it the same old way.*

3. *Create The Time*

   *To revisit your culture, and reassess your tone and atmosphere, testing the waters with your team. There is still time, and these strategies will be here when you and your team are ready.*

# CHAPTER 13

## TRUST

Trust is the proverbial "biggie." It is the deal breaker in almost all relationships; without trust, there is nothing. This is why it is of the utmost importance that your transformational leadership inspires innovation through the strategic creation of a culture of trust. If you create trust between leaders, trust with your employees, and trust with your customers, then you have a company poised for success.

Okay once again so simple to say, not so easy to do. And while we are going to talk about how to build trust, it is also your job, then, to retain it. Building trust the first time is challenging; building trust after it is lost is almost impossible.

Trust is more valuable in this economy, because it is far harder to come by. Right or wrong, we are living in distrustful times; we no longer automatically believe what we see or read. When Lehman brothers fell, with Wachovia not far behind it, our world as we know it started to change. Never before in our lifetimes had any of us witnessed dominant companies fail.

One day news reporters and politicians were saying the economy was up, then the next day reporting it was down; all that uncertainty lead us to stop looking for guarantees and to start looking for honesty, authenticity, and anything we felt we could control. As consumers, we stopped looking at what those in authority were saying about this economy, and started relying on what we knew we could count on: ourselves.

So in today's marketplace, so much more than our economy has changed, consumers have changed, we have changed, and so have our employees. Employees want to believe, they want to have trust and faith, but they are cautious to do so. Trust takes time to build, and creating an atmosphere of trust depends on your modes of communication, the patience you have, and the actions you take.

If you want your employees to take ownership, to fully engage, then you have to live, breathe, and communicate a culture of trust. Trust is a small word but an incredibly powerful one. It is important to note that when we define trust, it does not translate into words of security or guarantees. I believe that point is significant, because those are words full of promises we cannot keep, especially in today's economy. Creating trust within a culture is not about promising a positive outcome, or guaranteeing a job for life, it is simply about creating a culture of transparency and honesty.

## THE REAL WORLD

*When Joey Havens and his retiring predecessor began a one-year transition plan for the role of executive partner at Horne LLP, Joey did all the normal things an executive transitioning into this role would do: He focused on strategic issues, spent more time engaging with partners one-on-one, and found himself in a few more meetings.*

*Changing the leadership of a company is never easy, for leaders or the team. New leadership means new ideas, new ways of doing things, and some new level of uncertainty. Add to that fear of the unknown, as typically the only team members with intimate knowledge of what is really going on during the transition are the incoming and outgoing leadership.*

*Having already laid out the vision of the Wise Firm to the partner group, it was time to make a transformational shift in communication with the team. So Joey made the decision to take the mystery out of the executive partner transition. How? He started a blog, an internal, personal blog about what it was like to actually transition into the role of executive partner. Now, this was not some "surface" blog, where Joey shared only the facts and general updates; no, this was a blog that was real.*

*In post after post, Joey shared the good, the bad, and the ugly of the change in leadership. He made it a point to share his ransparency was shared with his team in a very open and personal way. He addressed what was easy and what was working, and, more importantly, what he was feeling about it all. He let the team in on how the partners worked through some of the challenges, handled disagreements, and found common ground to move forward.*

*The blog, meant to alleviate the mystery of the leadership transition, turned into a powerful tool to create a culture of trust. Why? Because Joey was so real in it, sharing the tough times, the unpleasant times, and the true challenges and rewards of being a leader.*

---

## BUILDING TRUST

I had a client reach out to me, she was worried about how to handle a difficult situation. She was not sure how to approach a conflict between her values and something her company was asking her to do. In a meeting with her boss, she learned she was being asked to do something she really did not believe in, and did not think would work.

Her company had just been through the second round of layoffs in less than a year. Understandably employee morale was low, and people were afraid for their jobs, for their friends and the future of the company.

To combat the issue, my clients executive leadership team had made the decision to hold a big team meeting, buy everyone pizza, and let every employee know that the layoffs were behind them and that their jobs were safe. Unfortunately, that was the same speech they had given the last time layoffs had occurred.

That is where my client's struggle was as she was being asked to say and support something she did not believe herself. Her boss had asked her to "sell" this concept to her team, get them to buy in and believe there would be no more layoffs. She was not sure she could do it, she was not sure she believed it, and she knew her team would not believe her. She wanted my help to figure out how to communicate this message and keep the trust she had built with her team.

I am guessing many of you, unfortunately, have been there. The problem is, people aren't stupid, especially not employees. My advice— if she wanted morale to stay high, if she wanted her team to believe in her, if she wanted to build trust—was to be honest. To be honest, she needed to be transparent about what her employees were facing, and what they could do about it.

To build trust, you have to be transparent, open, and honest with employees about what is going on: the good, the bad, and the ugly. Employees are not looking for, nor do they believe in, sunshine and roses. They want to trust that what their leaders are telling them is the truth, and that together they will find the solutions.

Let me relate this to your own world. How many of you believe politicians when they tell us our taxes will not go up at the same time telling us they will pay down the national debt? How many of you believe healthcare costs will stay flat, while our services will improve? None of you right? And how many of you would welcome the opportunity to vote for a politician who would be open, honest and truthful with us about the sacrifices we need to make and what needs to be done to put this country back on track?

Well I cannot do anything about finding a politician who is trustworthy, but I can help you become the type of leader that your team trusts.

## TRANSITION CLARITY

Once your team has the "lay of the land," they want to know what they (not you) can do about it. In other words, they want clarity. As we have discussed before, it is hard to believe, but 64% of performance-related issues come down to clarity: role clarity.

If employees just understand what is expected of them, what their priorities are, and where their time would be best spent supporting their team and moving their organization forward, employees will work harder and trust more.

We have talked endlessly about how, as a transformational leader, you need to be able to clearly articulate the vision of the company, but you also need to be able to clearly articulate the role each of your team members has in achieving that vision.

When trust is established, your team can break out of its old thought patterns, and be far more transparent with one another, more open with information and idea sharing. They will listen better and have more patience, and innovation will spark.

## THE TRANSFORMATIONAL-TRANSPARENT LEADER

So what does a transformational-transparent leader look like? You can't actually be transformational without being transparent, and to be transparent, you need to exhibit some specific qualities. Look at these characteristics to see how the transparent leader operates:

▸ They are predictable and consistent in communication, treatment of employees, etc.

▸ They are reliable, enabling everyone to trust them at their word.

▸ They "walk the walk" and uphold organizational visions, goals, or missions through such behaviors.

▸ They are open to new ideas and opinions from all employees; and they listen.

▸ They are patient and more than willing to work with employees to "connect the dots." For instance, a transparent leader has no problem taking the time to explain to an employee how their job figures into plans for overall success.

▸ They are always approachable and pursue interaction with employees at all levels.

▸ They accept and appreciate feedback about their performance.

▸ They are always accessible and ensure that all employees have the ability to get in touch.

▸ They treat everyone with interest, respect, and humility.

▸ Their communication skills are excellent, and they keep their entire team well informed in a timely manner.

▸ They do not lie when they cannot provide information, but instead indicate that they are unable to disclose details at the moment.

I did say that trust is not as easy as it might seem! That list represents a lot of qualities and behaviors, but I cannot emphasize enough that they must be in line with your own performance.

## IN THEIR OWN WORDS...

"Kelly Johnson... was one of the great airplane designers in history and... when it comes to inspiring innovation, we begin with Kelly and his famous '14 Rules and Practices'... His rules spell out a management approach heavy on collaboration and light on bureaucracy. They are designed for an industry that is fast, agile and driven. For example, one of Kelly's Rules was that: 'There must be mutual trust between the military project organization and the contractor... very close cooperation and liaison on a day-to-day basis.'"

- Lockheed Martin, 2013

## CLARIFYING CLARITY

While clarity is an important communication tool coming from the leader, make no mistake that as a transformational leader, you need to engage your employees in the process of clarity.

Once you are transparent about the "state of things" and you share your ideas on how the team can contribute, invite them to share. You need to get them engaged by actually engaging them. Employees don't need you to guarantee them a job or that your company will always be there. They just want to know where things stand, the opportunity to have a say in how to make them better and a role in the process.

### CALL TO ACTION

1. *Commit – Commit to creating a culture of trust, and realize that nothing can move forward without trust.*
2. *Embrace Transparency – Make a list or take an inventory of what your team needs to know and what you need to share.*

3. *Then Share - Be open and honest, and allow the team to question and give feedback.*

4. *Build Clarity – Revisit the vision, mission, and goals, over-communicate, and then give them a part in the process. Let them know what is most important, what you most need from them*

5. *Enjoy – Enjoy the process as you, a transformational leader, get ideas and solutions from your employees that are far better than any ideas you have ever had.*

*Keep in mind that creating a culture of trust also sparks innovation—and with innovation, you have opened the door for ownership at every level of your organization.*

*We have all heard phrases like "His team would lie down and die for him" or "They would follow her off the edge of a cliff." When your team is saying those things about you, you have created a culture of trust, and you are ready to open the door to ownership.*

*Keep in mind that creating a culture of trust also sparks innovation—and with innovation, you have opened the door for ownership at every level of your organization.*

*We have all heard phrases like "His team would lie down and die for him" or "They would follow her off the edge of a cliff." When your team is saying those things about you, you have created a culture of trust, and you are ready to open the door to ownership.*

# CHAPTER 14

## OWNERSHIP

Years ago, I was sitting in a very upscale professional office in Charlotte, North Carolina, waiting to speak to the CEO of a company. As usual, I arrived on time, but was asked to wait, as he was finishing up with clients. Not a problem; even though this was before cell phones and mobile access, I had learned to make good use of my time. I kept my briefcase packed with reading material,

---

### IN THEIR OWN WORDS...

"Leaders are accountable to assemble teams and lead them to optimal performance outcomes. An effective leader recognizes the importance of embracing differences in people and knows how to connect the dots amongst those differences to get the best outcomes from the team. This is what cultivates a workplace environment of continuous improvements, innovation and initiative. Leaders must foster a commitment from the team to embrace an innovation mindset where each employee learns to apply the differences that exist in one another for their own success and that of the organization."

- (Forbes, 2014)

books, articles, and research that I wanted to catch up on, and that I could find useful for my clients.

On this day, I ended up having more time than normal to read, and I put it to good use. I came across an article about leadership and John Chambers, the CEO of CISCO. Well, the article was not really about him, it was about the people who worked for him, and just how incredibly talented they were. The article said that each, in their own right, was perfectly qualified to be running their own businesses.

---

## IN THEIR OWN WORDS...

"I see this scenario often. 'How long will it take you to build this?' managers ask. 'Three weeks,' comes back the reply. And what's the first thing out of the manager's mouth? 'Can you do it in less?' And since they are the boss, and the developer might worry about his job, he says, 'Ok, two weeks.' Now who has ownership? The boss. Is the developer going to spend late nights getting it done? Not likely. Most people, when they are asked for something and commit to it themselves, they will do all they can to make it happen, because they have ownership."

- (Pixton, 2015)

---

That was the focus of the article, which posed the question of why, if these leaders were talented enough to be a CEO, why would they rather work at CISCO and for John (as they called him). The leaders of CISCO's reasoning? John Chambers created a work environment of ownership. Okay, that is not what the article said, but they described an environment where talented professionals were able to have say, and one in which they felt their voice was heard, and one where they felt responsible for the overall success of their ideas and the company. That culture of engagement was, for them, more fulfilling than being the CEO of their own company.

That one thing is the next strategy in creating an environment of engagement that leads to innovation: ownership. What is ownership? Ownership is the point at which you truly move from a heroic leader to a transformational leader. You still clearly set the direction, but you allow the team to determine how you will get there. Leadership is at this point a joint effort.

People support what they help create and what they feel a part of. As a leader, your job is to help your team understand the WHAT and the WHY of those goals that need to be accomplished, but you leave the question of HOW up to your team. It is in answering the HOW that the seeds of ownership are planted.

## TRUST AND THEN OWNERSHIP

Ownership is a focal point of this book, as this piece is significant in emotionally connecting employees while simultaneously empowering them. I am a strategist by training, and believe that focus and direction are critical to the overall success of any organization, but I would take a weak strategy developed by the people who have to implement it any day over a strong one driven top down.

Remember that I said ownership allows a company or individual to have something bigger than just goals. Ownership allows people to dream and set bigger visions for their futures. It gives them emotional ties to the work they do, as it becomes the conduit to realizing goals of any kind. It is the ultimate engagement.

Recall as well, that I pointed out four steps to ownership at the leadership level: personal investment, role recognition, alignment as a priority, and the recognition of and dedication to team and personal objectives. Employees need these too, and it is up to leadership to give them the tools essential for going through all four steps.

I also established that there are four levels of ownership: resistant, exempt, complying, and invested. It is important for you, as a leader, to become familiar with these levels and then use them to assess individuals, teams, and the company as a whole in terms of "where" you are with ownership. Thus, you have discovered that it is your job to give people and teams the resources needed for ownership, and that it is their role to act on all that has been communicated and given to them.

I want to clarify that point. As a leader, you can create a culture and provide the resources your team needs to take ownership, but whether or not they embrace it is up to them, the employees.

## SKIN IN THE GAME

The ultimate goal is to engage employees at all levels. To do that means giving them ownership and true "skin in the game." This requires that they have:

▶ Voice.

▶ Responsibility.

▶ Knowledge that their day-to-day work is actually a "piece of the action," whatever the action of your company might be.

Having a voice and responsibilities, and knowing that their job is recognized and essential, are sort of the unwritten new requirements of the workforce in the new economy.

That phrase above—"skin in the game"—is one more commonly used in the world of finance or leadership. Coined first by Warren Buffett, it was meant to describe scenarios in which "high-ranking insiders use their own money to buy stock in the company they are running" (Investopedia, 2015). For the purpose of this book and your culture, let's change out the term "money" for "ideas." When people use their own ideas, they are far more likely to ensure the plan succeeds, and that is ownership.

Now, company stock is a stake in the game, but we are not considering financial stakes here. Instead, we are looking at those different steps and resources for ownership, and how they might translate to "skin in the game" for employees and leaders. So, what is ownership? And how do voice and responsibility play a part here?

Well, if you have children, stubborn ones, and you have managed on occasion to get them to do what you want and need them to do, then you may very well have used the concept of ownership. If you have ever asked a child to eat their vegetables, they most likely said, "No." Then you might pull out the book of "manipulative parenting" and come up with off-the-wall ideas that "entice them" to want to choose to eat their vegetables.

My mother used the idea of asking me if I wanted to be a member of the clean plate club, and when I said, "Yes," she told me that membership meant I had to eat my vegetables. (I fell for that one until I was 11.) In that situation, I could or could not be a member—it was my choice, so I had ownership or "skin in the game." My brother, who was a bit more stubborn (and smarter), did not fall for the clean plate game, so she gave him a choice; rather than telling him to eat his vegetables, she simply asked if he would rather eat his peas or his carrots. When he chose carrots, he was in control. She gave us both a voice, a say, in how we were going to accomplish what she needed us to accomplish.

To create ownership, you have to give your team a voice; they need to have a say, an opinion, or an idea. The interesting thing is that you don't always even have to agree or even use their idea or their opinion—people just want to be asked and heard. Giving them voice (and listening) lets them know they matter, they are important, and that they are valued.

However, as a side note here, often the ideas and opinions you get are better than your own. Listen to your team, you may just be surprised at what you discover.

## IN THEIR OWN WORDS...

A Forbes article on ownership revealed a great deal about the impetus behind it, its benefits, and more: "Corporations have been leveraging the concept of ownership to motivate workers since the mid-1970s. During that time, the US workforce experienced an overall decline in productivity as workers became increasingly alienated and disengaged. Amidst these and other issues (e.g., the skyrocketing number of workers eligible for Social Security benefits), the US Congress passed legislation incentivizing the sale of company stock to current employees, giving birth to the employee stock ownership plan.

The idea was simple—give workers a piece of the pie and they will work harder and be happier, right? Turns out, not so much. As stock ownership plans rolled out across the nation, organizational researchers conducted a number of studies with mixed and inconclusive results. Some studies found slight positive effects on productivity while others found no difference at all. One large study even found that the amount of stock ownership had no relationship to an employee's level of commitment or job satisfaction.

In response to these underwhelming findings, a group of researchers found that the feeling of ownership mattered more than actual ownership when it came to predicting attitudes and behaviors. In other words, even the most well-conceived employee stock ownership plan would fail unless it was implemented in such a way that employees experienced greater feelings of ownership towards their job and company."

## RESPONSIBILITY

One of the greatest benefits of being a transformational leader versus a heroic one is that the job of ensuring success of the organization is now not all up to you. When you give your team voice, when you create a culture of ownership, you also transfer responsibility; you give them "skin in the game" for ensuring that the goals are reached, the mission is accomplished, and the team succeeds.

One of the biggest problems associated with lack of employee engagement is the time, money, and resources lost on blame. Whether we are blaming the economy, leadership, or the customers, it is lost time, it is wasted time, and it is time we will never get back. It is time that that would be better spent coming up with ideas and solutions to succeed.

When you give the team a voice, you ensure that the ideas needed to move the organization forward, get past obstacles, and grow the business are their ideas or at least partly theirs. When the ideas are theirs, they own the solutions, and with that they will take responsibility for ensuring it succeeds: doing what it takes to work hard, make changes, and not lose precious time complaining about what isn't working, instead putting their time and energy into what is.

## TRANSFORMATIONAL LEADERS AND OWNERSHIP

So how do you lead this way? What needs to be different in your leadership style? How do you ensure you communicate that you want the team involved, but that you are still in charge? You need to learn to lead through the power of the question.

## LEADING THROUGH QUESTIONS

Let me explain. Years ago I worked for a boss who had a huge and very positive impact on my career and my life. Like most people who impact you at this level, he was simultaneously the most inspiring and frustrating person I have ever worked for, which turned out to be a great combination. In fact, that is exactly what you ought to look for in a leader, if you want to grow as an individual and grow in your career, as I did.

Jeff was (and I am sure still is) amazing at a lot of things, but his real gift was in developing people. His inspiration and encouragement allowed you to take risks and try new things; his confidence and belief made it safe to fail and make mistakes. In the time I worked with him,

I learned quite a bit, but the most important lesson I learned from him was the power of a question.

And the power of the question was exactly why Jeff was so frustrating. Because no matter how much you begged or pleaded, no matter how stuck you were, he would never, and I mean never, give you the answer. He always, always answered any question you asked him with a question. No matter what problem, challenge, or situation you came to him with, he always answered your questions by asking you the two most important questions in leadership: "Why do you feel we should do that?" and "How do you think it should work?"

He was like a broken record, always repeating the same two questions. In fact, he did this so consistently, he even frustrated his kids. One time I went to his office with an issue, and his five-year-old daughter Caroline was visiting. As I explained my situation to Jeff, Caroline listened, and when he, true to form, answered my question, he did so by asking me what I thought. Caroline sighed and said, "Oh daddy, do you do that to them too!" Apparently Jeff was not only raising leaders at work, but he was raising leaders at home too!

They are pretty simple questions, ones that are so incredibly effective when it came to leading and developing a team. Why? Because, by asking these two simple questions consistently and routinely, Jeff was able to reduce his need to be involved in the day-to-day operations of the team (allowing him to use his talents to grow market share, enhance client experience, and stay on top of changing market conditions), as well as consistently and continually developing talent at each and every level of his organization. This made us a strong, effective, and very profitable team. By asking these two questions routinely and consistently, he was able to transform from manager to leader, ensuring not only the growth of his company, but the development and growth of his team.

When you lead through questions, like Jeff did, you expand your leadership abilities to become a business coach, mentor, and sales leader, creating and building a team that is ready for anything and ready for today's constantly shifting market place. The power of leadership through questions creates a team that is:

1. **Solution-Oriented:** We learned early on never to go to Jeff without thinking our situation through, analyzing the problem, and coming up with possible scenarios and solutions for how best to fix it.

2. **Drama-Free:** We quit going to Jeff with minor complaints or issues with employees or customers; we would keep him in the loop, but we learned early on that if we didn't have it fixed by the time it got to his door, we would fix it (ourselves) while we were in there.

3. **Ownership-Driven:** Since the solutions and ideas were ours, we took pride in them and responsibility for ensuring their success We grew from sales associates to sales leaders, embracing our goals and working together to build our market share.

4. **Thinking & Doing:** His leadership through questions created team members that not only had the ability to do, but to think. We grew not only in our skill level, but also in our ability to problem-solve and critically think.

5. **Interdependent, not dependent**: The result of a "questioning approach" was a team that could stand on their own as individuals and as a team. We were a strong team, but we did not miss a beat or lose a step when one of our members moved on or was promoted. We were interdependent (working well together), but not dependent on a member or a strong leader.

Leadership does not have to be complicated, but it does have to be effective. Taking a "question" approach is a great step to ensuring that you, as a leader, are many things, including a business coach. As a business coach, you ensure that you are giving your team the room they need to grow and develop, while taking risks, embracing failure, and building their confidence to become leaders themselves.

## STIMULATING OWNERSHIP

Now is the moment to emphasize and strategically use the autonomy methods you have created, giving employees the trust and option to use their own judgment and decision making to do their clearly defined jobs. Additionally, this is the moment to be sure that they have a solid role or identity in their work, and that they will see things through from beginning to end.

The simplest ways to stimulate ownership include:

▶ Eliminating management methods that limit autonomy, including multiple-approval processes, heavy monitoring or supervision, and using "directives" instead of "dialogues."

▶ Finding ways of involving employees when making decisions that have an impact or influence on their work.

▶ Allowing and encouraging employees to use their own judgment and problem-solving skills, and creating a safe space to make mistakes or wrong decisions.

▶ Ensuring that your employees have many opportunities to complete any tasks or work they begin.

▶ Making it very clear that each employee's work contributes towards the outcome, as this allows him or her to see that their work fits into a bigger picture.

▶ Engaging employees by involving them in all aspects of the work, including the planning, reporting, and assessing/evaluating.

▶ Rewarding and recognizing each and every decision they make, to incent the behavior you want.

This list describes a new type of relationship between leader and employee, one that gives them a stake in the outcome and "skin in the game." It is also the point at which all the work you have done, all the investment in changing your leadership style, begins to pay off, the point at which you start to see true return on investment for being a transformational leader.

In my book Winning in the Trust & Value Economy, I related a story about a web developer who lost a gig because he was unable to deliver on his brand promise. As the owner of the firm, with a staff to support his goals, it was clear that he and his team were not on the same page, did not know who they were and what values to put as priority. The result was failure. The important thing to learn from this is example, is that it was failure not because of a lack of talent, skill, or ability, but because of a lack of Transformational Leadership and ownership of the team.

This point proves the incredible value of knowing what your employees need: a bigger purpose, specific values to follow, and clarity on their role. Knowing who they are and how that aligns with your goals will amp up performance exponentially.

## CALL TO ACTION

*Your next steps are to create opportunities to give your employees a voice:*

1. *Create Opportunities – Make opportunities such as team meetings, project teams, or problem-solving committees. Provide employees with an opportunity to state their opinions and their ideas for doing things better.*

2. *Take Action - Then you need to let them do it! In other words, give them responsibility to decide how the work will get done, how the goal will be reached, and who will do what.*

3. *Lead through Questions* – *Understand that even as they take ownership, they will struggle with not falling back into their own comfort zone of turning to you for solutions and answers. As a leader, you need to learn to lead through the power of the question. The more you ask, the more your team will think, the more solutions they will come up with, the more ideas they will have, the more responsibility they will take, and the more skin in the game they will have.*

# CHAPTER 15

## PERFORMANCE

n 2008, the year we first began to feel the impact of this changing economy, I was asked to give a keynote presentation for a healthcare organization. The focus was to be on how to motivate and inspire employees in a down-turning economy.

---

### IN THEIR OWN WORDS...

"I recently met with the CEO of a major business in Australia and discussed their need to revamp and humanize their performance management process (their employees referred to their performance appraisal process as a 'drive by shooting'). While the business was performing well, they had high turnover and were struggling to attract great people.

As we discussed a simpler, more coaching-based performance process, I saw the fear in his eyes. 'What if people start goofing off around here?' I told him that part of building a great company is building trust—trust in leaders, trust in managers, and trust in employees. Not always an easy thing for a hard-driving CEO to accept."

- (Bersin, 2015)

Now, I knew I could go with the tried-and-true methods, such as reward and recognition programs, incentives etc., but I wanted more. I wanted to understand what really inspires and taps into an employee's intrinsic motivation. So I set off to do some intensive research and really understand not only what inspires motivation, but what sustains their motivation. What I learned surprised me; I discovered that although reward, recognition, and money provided a nice little boost to employee morale, those were not the things that were exactly what "motivated" people when times get tough.

I discovered the two things employees wanted most: to clearly understand what was expected of them, and to be held accountable—yes, to be held accountable. In other words, they want you to manage their performance. Why? Because employees want most of all to do a good job and to be successful. Beyond that, they want support and training from their leaders. Employees, actually want you to provide the tools and resources they need so they can perform to the best of their ability, and help the organization be successful. They also want to know that their leaders will hold them accountable, reward them for a job well done, and provide consequences when they do not.

Employees most want leaders who closely manage performance, create engagement, make tough decisions and inspire innovation. Employees want leaders who do this, because they provide the only type of security you can truly have in this type of economy, an environment where everyone will pull their weight and work together, where those who do not will no longer be members of the team. When leaders hold team members accountable, employees have peace of mind that those who are under performing cannot hurt the overall performance of the team, or hurt the company's opportunity to achieve their goals and complete their mission.

## MANAGING PERFORMANCE

"Managing performance" is such a bland term for such an important concept, as it relates to engagement and innovation. If you want employees to engage, if you want them to invest in you and your organization, you have to invest in them.

Managing performance is about creating the right balance of support and accountability, and the key is balance. Here are five strategies to keep yourself and your team in check.

Ask Permission – You cannot even begin to manage performance until you get to know your team, and understand what they know and do not know from a skill perspective. Before you can train your team, you need to coach your team. You need to invest the time to learn about them—who they are, what drives them, what does not—and, in essence, build a relationship that grants you permission to lead. Yes, you want "permission" to lead them, correct and reward their behavior, and teach them new skills. Sure, you have the right (after all you are their boss), but having the right does not lead to engaging your employees. If you want to manage performance correctly, you must first understand that this is far more powerful when done from the position of coach rather than dictator.

Celebrate Forward Movement – Not everyone progresses at the same rate or the same level, so don't just celebrate the winners; celebrate each and every member of your team for the progress they are making. As long as they are going forward, they are showing you that they are putting an effort in, continuing to try, and staying the course. The more, as a leader, you support forward movement, the more forward movement you will see. So sure, celebrate the big ones and the strong performers, but don't forget the rest of the team and those just starting out or those who are new to the game. Help them to transform by paying attention and being genuinely enthusiastic about each forward step they take, no matter how small.

Develop Skills & Talents – To engage team members, we have to give them opportunities to grow, learn, and develop, and that means training. I know, in this day and age I am supposed to call it something more politically correct, like "learning environment," "skill enhancement," or something else more progressive, but honestly, at the end of the day, it is training. When you engage the right people, they come complete with the right attitude, drive, and desire to learn—you just need to fill the gaps and provide the opportunities to train the skills they need to learn. When you develop your team and build their skills, they not only get better at their jobs, but they also gain confidence and belief in themselves, all of which comes back to you and your organization ten-fold.

Learn to Love Accountability – Shift your paradigm and embrace the concept. You will love accountability and so will your team when you use it correctly. Accountability is about learning what actions your people are taking, and what results they are getting from those actions. Armed with that information, you can help your team understand where they are doing well, and where they are struggling. Accountability, at its best, is a learning tool. You can understand where and how your team members are spending their time wisely and where they are wasting it, along with what specific actions are getting them results, and what are not. You have exactly the information you need to help them become more effective and efficient at their jobs. What can be more motivating than that? Accountability is nothing more than a tool to help people consistently improve, and when you use that tool correctly, you will see them transform.

Dive Deep on Non-Performance – Separate lack of skills or knowledge from discipline issues. Nothing is more demotivating to a group of people (or any team, for that matter) than working with or alongside team members who are clearly not doing the work, and then having a leader who does not address the situation. Your team wants to be successful, and they realize it takes each and every member of the team to be fully engaged to do that. As transformational leaders, it is our job to help our teams stay motivated, by diving deep on performance issues. We need to understand if lack of performance is skill-based (and if it is, then coach and support the individual) or discipline-based. If it is a discipline problem, then one of the strongest ways to create an environment of engagement and innovation is to address discipline issues quickly, strongly, and with complete confidentiality.

It may be hard to believe, but it is true: Your team is seeking accountability and performance management. They want you to notice what they do, correct them if they are wrong, and help them to grow and learn. In fact, they cannot engage without it.

## THE REAL WORLD

*As part of the ongoing journey of building the Wise Firm, Joey Havens and the leadership team of HORNE asked for feedback about what the firm associates saw as the most important issue the firm needed to deal with, or take advantage of, in order to take the firm to the next level.*

*The "directions" were no more detailed than that, as representatives from across the firm gathered in live sessions to share their insights. There were no boundaries, no right or wrong, just their honest opinions and feedback on what issue, if focused on with intent, could move the organization forward. The answer was one the leadership team never saw coming, and one they never thought would be what the team would ask for.*

*The one thing the team asked to focus on, the one thing they felt would have the most power and the most impact if the firm could correct was conflict avoidance. That meant that, in order to move the firm forward, their culture needed to be marked by an understanding of how to immediately, skillfully, and consistently deal with conflict in a healthy way.*

*The team clearly shared that they wanted to be told when things are not going well, or how they could be doing better in their job, and they wanted to be able to voice their ideas and opinions that may "conflict" with others' without fear of repercussion. In response, the HORNE's leadership team made dealing with conflict avoidance a major focal point of the firm. Specifically, the entire firm is dedicated to becoming skilled at receiving feedback well. Conflict avoidance, they believe, will dissipate when team members are skilled at not only giving, but also skilled at receiving feedback.*

*Consider that Entrepreneur's annual "Great Place to Work Rankings" often describes companies where "people actually seek accountability and act as owners of the business... [and] believe management trusts them without looking over the shoulder and 92% say they are given a lot of responsibility."*

*"Looking over the shoulder," i.e. micromanagement is not what we are talking about with performance management, as it is something that disengages workers in any economy. After all, micromanagement expresses a distinct lack of trust. "If management doesn't track your every move, the work may not get done" is the ultimate message employees receive when micromanaged.*

What is the new economy's method of gauging performance? We have already looked at this from a few angles, but let's just face it head on.

## THE POWER OF ACCOUNTABILITY

Accountability is not about punishment. It is about discovering where employees are on the learning curve, and building a framework that includes all of the support employees need to engage and succeed. Accountability is about ensuring employees have what they need to do their jobs to the best of their ability; it is about investing in them to ensure they have the tools and feedback to consistently improve.

Through learning we understand if our employees are doing incredibly well, if they have a skill development issue, or if they are just not doing their job. How we, as leaders, handle those issues, are very different! Unfortunately, many tend to shy away from accountability, and while they may reward and recognize employees who are doing well, leaders tend to fall short in the areas of developing skills and dealing with those team members not pulling their weight.

## THE COST OF NO ACCOUNTABILITY

Partners in Leadership did a survey about the price for lack of accountability and found some astonishing figures. For example, the percentages of respondents who admitted to behaving in unproductive behaviors were immense, and included such patterns as "covering their trail" (93%), "blaming others" (88%), and "ignoring the problems" (68%). The pattern, though, shows many people stuck doing something more like "waiting around" than digging into responsibilities and delivering results.

Imagine the workplace in which employees are comfortable with a bit of autonomy because they know precisely what is expected and have the resources to do it, when all that is left is for them to give it their best effort. Of course, they will take ownership and engage, and they will automatically live up to the accountability required for the job.

That is entirely different from waiting for the proverbial ball to drop and then looking for someone to blame. When this new approach becomes a pattern throughout the entire team or organization, you can only imagine the improvements in productivity, not to mention the creation of a more enjoyable place to work.

As I have said several times, though, you will not put "accountability" at the top of the "to-do list" and have it manifest within a day or two. However, many of the steps you will take throughout this book can begin to create a culture of accountability in the workplace, or begin to lay a solid foundation for one.

## THE NEED FOR FEEDBACK, EVALUATIONS, AND FOLLOW-UP

As one of the hidden benefits of creating a culture of accountability, when you create a culture of accountability, employees will seek feedback rather than wait for it. Remember that report from Entrepreneur? It noted that in the best workplaces, employees seek out feedback and want to be held accountable. They seek it because, one, they do not fear it; and two, feedback nurtures their desire to improve and take ownership.

To create a culture of accountability, there must be channels for feedback and evaluation; channels they can access and they can access from the bottom up. Note that I wrote channels, plural. This is because employees will want different types of feedback, and will want feedback on different things. Who and how they ask to evaluate them on their leadership skills may be different from who provides feedback on their knowledge of operational efficiency.

Make evaluation an expectation and dialogues a mutually beneficial activity, and employees will engage eagerly in the process and in your organization. Note that for employees actively seeking feedback, this process eliminates one more "to do" from the heroic leader's list.

I do not know one heroic leader who looks forward to performance reviews. Why? Because they are a burden, something you do once a year that focuses on a set of accomplishments someone else determined were important. Performance reviews are not a true dialogue in which both parties are eager to share and eager to learn, in which both want to be involved in the process.

## ENGAGEMENT AND PERFORMANCE

There is a four-part strategy for increasing engagement and inspiring innovation as it relates to performance, and you have to include all parts to truly accomplish your goal:

1. Feedback - This is about expectations, goals, obstacles, needed improvements, and more. However, feedback should not be one-sided, and it should include feedback from employee to leadership about these same issues.

2. Growth and Learning - Analyst Josh Bersin identified five factors that increase engagement. They include the work, the management environment, inclusion and flexibility in the workplace, trust and meaning from leadership, and the ability to learn and grow. If feedback is about improvement and learning, it presents a key opportunity for growth, and even excellence.

3. Integrity - Doing what you (as leadership or employee) commit to is a major area of performance.

4. Embrace Failure – This can be summed up by making it okay for a team member to try and to fail. Innovation is the creation of new ideas, new ways of doing things, and creative solutions to tough problems. If you want to inspire innovation, you have to embrace failure and create a safe culture for it to exist.

When performance is assessed as a dialogue, as management of objectives, or as a learning opportunity, it sheds most of its negative reputation. There is a lot of power to be delivered into employees' hands when you offer support and accountability as the ultimate means to higher performance in the new economy.

## CALL TO ACTION

1. *Clearly Define - Establish a clear definition of performance management for your company, and share the definition and expectation with your team.*

2. *Strike the Balance - Work with your leader to strike the balance of performance, ensuring you and they are clear on the balance of support and accountability.*

3. *Redefine - Redefine accountability within your organization, and ensure that it is a tool to support learning and growth, not to catch people doing something wrong.*

4. *Separate - Separate skill development issues and discipline issues; provide opportunity for skills training and learning, and handle discipline issues well with the right type of discipline.*

*Allowing employees to succeed in what they are doing is the same as ensuring they feel their own competence. Few people will turn away from work that makes them feel that they are competent, yet which still gives them room to grow, innovate, and learn.*

*When you build a culture of trust, encourage ownership, and make performance a part of the job rather than something upon which an employee is scrutinized, judged, or even threatened, things change radically. Your workforce, when exposed to these strategies, will engage positively, willingly, and whole-heartedly. There will be little that impedes progress, because your workplace is one designed to nurture innovation, one that offers a positive culture and shows employees that they are at the top of the list of priorities.*

*With the mention of the word "top," it is an ideal time to review all that we have learned about engagement and innovation and discover how these things put everyone at the very top—the customers, the employees, and leadership.*

# CHAPTER 16

## GETTING TO THE TOP – TRUST, OWNERSHIP, PERFORMANCE

I t is lonely at the top! That is a cliché, but there is some solid truth to it, don't you think? Everything has shifted quickly, and though there are classic leadership responsibilities you must still meet, your role has also expanded to include becoming chief employee engagement officer, master of market trends, and new customer magnet.

The level to which you are skilled as a leader to attract, retain, and fully engage your employees is the key to determining how successful you are going to be. Yet with all the research, articles, and information published out there, enormous portions of the global workforce are still disengaged. Indifferent, unconcerned, and unsatisfied, they are not meeting their own goals, and most definitely not helping their employers to meet the company's goals. Thus, the task of turning this around sits firmly on the shoulders of leadership.

Having completed the previous chapters, you now have a much clearer understanding of your role as a leader in the new economy. You know that your plans and objectives include creating trust, encouraging ownership, and using performance in ways you may have never even considered before. These strategies are somewhat complex in the abstract, but when you compare the ideal against your current working model, it is easy to see the biggest gaps or weaknesses.

## YOUR CURRENT REALITIES AND THE POSSIBILITIES

Trust must come first. Without slowing down and building trust first, all other strategies will be on very shaky ground at best. We now understand that while trust needs to come first, it cannot be sustained without the strategies that follow.

Changes in your leadership include creating transparency, offering support, clarifying roles, giving purpose to individuals and teams, communicating in dialogue over dictation, encouraging innovation, establishing accountability and ownership, and more.

In taking steps to bring these strategies and policies to life, you are going to begin to build trust automatically. You become the credible, dependable, and positively predictable "boss." You show that personal and professional growth is encouraged and that respect is a major emphasis at all times. You are committed to moving from a heroic leader to a transformational leader, a leader under whom his team can also move from entitled to engaged employees.

By implementing so many changes to help meet the needs of employee engagement initiatives, you are also laying the foundation for ownership. As noted in one report from Forbes, "Enforcing accountability is a key component to sustaining performance momentum. However, when you can give your employees 'ownership' in the process of defining how accountability is enforced, you inspire trust and a desire to go above and beyond the call of duty."

Thus, you see that there is an interdependency between all of the strategies. Without one, you may find it hard to implement another. Working on trust-building leads to ownership; creating opportunities for ownership builds trust; encouraging accountability leads to performance momentum; and establishing evaluation as part of the day-to-day supports performance and growth.

So things are challenging, but they may not be as demanding as you initially believe. You won't have to work forever building a system for employee engagement. Instead, you will put to use the strategies we have considered throughout these chapters, and in doing so, you will create a foundation and framework that will do most of the work (now and in the future) for you.

That foundation and framework, though, will include employees and teams. As fully engaged employees, they will help your company meet goals or missions, in addition to growing new leaders, expanding the organization, and removing some of the biggest stressors from your shoulders.

Also, keep in mind that initiating the whole process is simple. Simply ask yourself:

▸ Where are we in terms of a culture of trust? What can I do right now to begin building that essential trusting environment? Remember, trust is built through transparency and clarity.

▸ Do the employees, managers, and local-level leaders feel any sort of ownership? Can they each say that their work/job is "theirs"? What needs to be done to begin encouraging all employees to feel ownership?

▸ Is performance about results and not about how those results are reached? What can the company do right away to realign performance to growth? How can performance become part of "making things happen" rather than responding to "bad things that happen"?

If we summed it all up into a single question, it might be as simple as, "What are we doing to empower employees?"

## EMPOWERED AND ENGAGED

After all, empowered employees tend to be those who are engaged, and those who use that power to experience the kind of deeper meaning, professional growth, and purpose that so many desire.

And when the workforce is engaged? We have already discovered that companies with the greatest levels of engagement tend also to be the most successful. Putting employees as the priority is likely to put your firm at the top. Customers are direct beneficiaries of your engagement programs too, since engaged employees make the discretionary effort to deliver premium customer service.

This gives the consumers in the new economy something they desire almost above all—connection. They feel connected to your brand, your team, and your organization. They sense they are not a dollar sign or just an account number, but an actual customer given attention and spending their money or time with an organizaiton that they can trust. Yes, they can trust you, because you value them! Welcome to the new economy!

So, employees on the top put customers at the top, and this brings your business to a whole new level, too—yes, right at the top!

Initially, it does seem like a lot of work to begin analyzing and altering the approaches that your company (and you) take to accomplish such major issues, but the rewards are well worth the effort. And when you take these steps, your leadership becomes much stronger.

As the simplest illustration of this, everything that you do to build trust, encourage ownership, and use performance differently is going to undo damages of micromanagement.

Teams that have suffered under years of this sort of leadership tend to have what many call "learned helplessness." They are not accountable, they don't have to worry about failure, and they need only to "do their work and go home." They are totally disengaged and relatively indifferent.

Applying the different strategies for trust, ownership, performance, innovation, and engagement re-educates your workforce. Their learned

## IN THEIR OWN WORDS...

"The secret recipe to inspiring employees is to know the 'ingredients' of the people you are inspiring. People want to know that their leaders understand their tendencies, aptitudes and behaviors well-enough to best work with and motivate them. The best leaders and coaches always do.

When you spend time with your employees, make it matter. Don't just expect your time and title to inspire them. Employees want a leader that pays attention and genuinely cares about them.

Great leaders take the time to know the ingredients before they can create the best recipe for success. Employees are most inspired when a leader takes the time to know them and show that they have their best interests at heart.

Leaders that know how to prepare thousands of recipes are those who continually make the ingredients better—and keep them from spoiling."

- (Llopis, 2013)

helplessness is replaced by accountability, performance, purpose, drive, and many other key behaviors. Employees see pathways before them for learning, opportunities for leadership, and creativity. They are more than happy to use discretionary effort, because they understand that it benefits everyone involved.

Your strategies become the common system at work too. For example, in this new approach to the workplace, there is room for mistakes and failure, which are essential for growth. However, you also have strong mechanisms in place for catching things early, and engaging the team in problem solving and solution creation. There are connections that guide leaders and employees along a much more stable path, creating trust and driving ownership and innovation.

As one writer indicated, "This requires investment in building trust and it takes time—but these investments will reward leaders with bold new ideas, better performance, and commitment to the business" (FastCompany, 2015).

---

## CALL TO ACTION

1. *At this point, you as the leader have the basic information needed to assess the company and your leadership, to recognize where they might be failing, and to provide employees with the resources essential to engagement, innovation, and organizational growth.*

2. *It is time to break our leadership habits, habits that have you caught in the heroic leadership trap, a trap that ensures you remain overworked, stressed out, and burdened with the responsibility of trying (and failing) to engage your team.*

3. *This is a marathon, not a sprint, so do not expect change overnight. Make a commitment now to reread this section of the book and continue to build skills that fully engage your team and create ownership at every level and innovation at every turn.*

*Leadership is a skill that touches so many areas that it produces a domino effect depending on which style of leadership you implement. Embrace your heroic leader and you will fall backwards; embrace your transformational and you will fall forward.*

---

## AS YOU FINISH PART TWO

It may seem difficult to make such sweeping changes in your

approaches to leadership and the subsequent changes these will demand within your organization, but they are essential. You should not think of them as something you have to do, but as something you understand that, while tough on the front end, yield a strong and long-lasting rate of return on the back end.

## THE REAL WORLD

*My nephew, Cab, spent a semester of school in Patagonia in a NOLS (National Outdoor Leadership School) leadership program. I know tough life! The goal of the semester and the NOLS leadership program is to spend a semester learning hands-on what it takes to truly be a leader: making tough decisions, calculating risk, handling adversity, inspiring leadership in others, establishing leadership at every level, and the list goes on.*

*The program lasted from September through mid-December, and for that entire time, he was completely cut off from the "real world", no phone, no text, no Internet, and not even a letter to let us know where he was or how he was doing. To add to the challenge, the conditions were tough: Half the semester was spent on a glacier with wind chills well below freezing; the second half was spent day-in, day-out sea-kayaking, responsible all his own supplies, and living on only what he could carry. To say the least, this was probably more than a leadership course; it was a true study in the human condition.*

*When he returned home, I was anxious to hear about the trip, what he had learned, and how he had changed. After giving him congratulatory hugs, kissing him more than any 19-year-old wants to be kissed by his aunt, and wading through all of his photos and funny stories, I asked him to go for a hike so we could talk. I wanted to learn what he had gained from his experience. As I listened to him, I saw a different kid in front of me; his passion and depth of understanding had transformed him from a teenager into a leader.*

*The list of his accomplishments and lessons learned was long and varied, but it was more how he learned than what he learned that caught my attention. See, the counselors took the roles of advisor and supporter, allowing the leader within the student to emerge (or not) from the group. They created the culture and set the tone, giving the group advice and thoughts on how they should lead, but that, for the most part, is where their interference stopped and where the groups and individuals struggle to lead began. While the group was given plenty of information, the actual decision on what to do and how to do it was ultimately theirs, and so were the rewards and consequences of their decisions. It was in the rewards and consequences that the learning truly happened, and the leader within ultimately emerged.*

Let me give you an example: Three of the best lessons that Cab, my nephew, walked away with, both in terms of what he learned and how he learned them, are as follows:

## EASY NOW – HARD LATER

This one is my favorite. This lesson is, as a leader, you have decisions to make and work to get done. Whether you do it now or whether you do it later, the decisions and choices are still there. However, doing them now is often EASY, while putting them off until later can result in those very decisions being HARD, harder than they have to be, anyway. Cab quickly learned this one the hard way. While hiking in severe conditions, the counselors said that, despite the cold, the intense hiking combined with carrying 50-pound packs would mean they would work up a sweat and their clothes would get wet. To avoid rashes, athlete's foot, and small rub burns, the counselors suggested they take their socks off at night and let them dry out. Now, this sounds like a smart idea, and it is, but you have to remember that it was freezing. The first night, Cab elected not to do this, which was Easy Now. The result was a painful, long, and very uncomfortable hike the following day. With small blisters and a rash forming on his feet, he learned the meaning of Hard Later.

This is a great lesson. Think of the times as a leader when you knew an employee or a client was a challenge, but you procrastinated on a decision. Did the delay make it any easier? No. Putting it off took what could have been easy now and made it hard later!

## IN THEIR OWN WORDS...

"'I have my work life and my home life. They don't mix.' We've had a number of managers try and tell us this. We quickly call BS when we hear it. Two separate lives? That's called 'multiple personality disorder.' If we are disengaged at work, it's pretty tough to make the switch to an engaged home life. We're simply not wired that way. DecisionWise research shows that engaged employees are far more likely to be engaged outside of work as well."

- (Decision-Wise, 2015)

### PREPARED AND FLEXIBLE

Before the course started, all participants were advised to arrive in shape, both mentally and physically. This was not an adventure where you could fake it until you made it. Luckily, this is one lesson that Cab paid attention to, but unfortunately, several of his team members did not. Getting in shape mentally and physically, Cab made sure he was prepared for conditions and events that were beyond his comprehension, which gave him the confidence to be flexible and to understand that sometimes his value to the group was as a leader and others as simply a strong member of the team.

Those in the group who were not prepared became a drain on the group, both in terms of the extra support and help they needed, and in terms of their lack of confidence and their fear. This affected their flexibility, which hurt morale and the group's overall ability to achieve.

So I ask: Are your leaders prepared? Do they invest in training and development, beyond what you provide? Do they need to build confidence? What is their commitment to growth, and their flexibility to teach when called to do so and learn from others when the situation requires?

## ENJOY AND ALIGN

The last lesson was never told to Cab, but rather one he figured out on his own through a strong role model—the most powerful way to learn. One of his guides was from India, and he was Cab's favorite, because Cab said no matter what, this guide was always happy. If the weather was really bad, he would laugh and sing through it; if the trail was tough, he would tell a story to distract the group; and when crisis struck, he would always look to find the opportunity and focus his energy there.

Cab learned and began to practice what this masterful guide had taught him, while you cannot control what happens, you can control how you react to it—how you react impacts the team, their productivity, and their overall experience. This information is vital in our Trust & Value Economy. And Cab learned that when he chose to enjoy leadership, no matter the conditions, and align himself with like-minded individuals, he had more fun, accomplished so much more, and was more confident and proud of who he was and what he had done. He emerged as a leader who could not only excel at meeting a goal, but one who could inspire others to get there, too, and to go beyond their limits.

So I ask: Are these the traits you look for in leaders? And, as a leader, what type of leader are you? How do you handle tough situations and pressure? How do you lead your team through it?

Again, this was an amazing experience, both in terms of what Cab accomplished and, more so for me, the innovative style in which he was taught to lead. This was so much more powerful than learning from the masters' best practices and top skills. Instead, he was given the skills to succeed, the support to try, and the room to fail. He was given ownership, a voice, skin in the game, and he held accountable both by his leaders and by nature (the ultimate teacher.)

Statistics (which I have already offered in abundance) have proven that engaged employees pave the way for their companies to succeed. They put the customer as a priority, and they see the company's success and their own as one in the same.

One of the biggest lessons you should gain from this section is that leadership needs to be connected. It needs to be connecting and getting "in touch" at all levels—in touch with employees, customers, and your own leadership style.

And what about the role of the employee? This is the missing link, the forgotten part of most employee engagement programs? To truly create a culture of employee engagement, one that inspires innovation and gets your team to step to the plate and own it, you need to give your employees a part to play. Yes, they need "skin in the game"!

# PART III

## EMPLOYEES – THE MISSING LINK

U nlike most employee engagement books or programs that focus only on the organization and its leadershipand what they need to do or change in order to create an effective employee engagement program; this book incorporates the employee. It is important to remember that the critical component to foster employee engagement is the employee. No matter how great a leader you are, how transformational you have become, you do not have the skills, the power, or the charisma to force or motivate an employee to engage. That choice remains with the individual.

This is what I refer to as the missing link, the piece of the puzzle that has been left out. If you want to engage your employees, if you want them to get more focused, more efficient, and more effective, then take a look at what is missing in your employee-engagement process—the employee. Oh, we think we "involve" the employee because we put them on committees, ask their opinion, and hold "town meetings" to ensure our employees participate in open communication forums. However, there is a very thin line between telling people to get engaged and actively involving them in the engagement process. And it is that thin line that holds the key, the secrets, and the missing link that actually engages them, leading to increased profitability, morale, and customer satisfaction. People support what they help create, and we need to understand that engagement is not something we can do for other people; it is a personal choice they need to make. And the employee that chooses to engage is the one that is in control of their own future, and the one that companies strive to keep.

The process of becoming the employee that companies strive to keep is truly the reason I wrote this book. I wanted employees to understand that even in uncertain times, and shifting economic conditions, there are things they can do to feel in control and in charge of their career. In today's economy, I have spoken with and experienced so many employees who are basically paralyzed, frozen in some sort of fear. They fear that they will lose their jobs, that they will not find another, that the weight of "doing more with less" will become too much, and that they have lost control of their professional and personal lives.

The reality is nothing could be further from the truth, and in part three, the last section of this book, we are going to lay out for you exactly what you need to get back in control of your career and your life, becoming the employee that companies strive to keep. This is the very essence of redefining responsibility and seeing it not as a burden, but rather the path to power, freedom, and purpose.

Whether you are an employee, who is reading this in order to learn how to improve engagement, or the employer trying to see things through the employee's perspective; this part of the book is going to give the details employees need to begin creating their own culture of engagement. This book will both provide you with the knowledge and the inspiration to stop waiting for something or someone else to do it for you.

In the end, employees will better understand precisely how and why engagement is of such tremendous benefit to them directly. This holds true whether their work environment cultivates engagement or not!

Take a moment and reflect, do you remember the statistics about employee engagement programs? They are costing billions in lost revenues and related costs, yet we continue to do them with no change in their effectiveness in site. So, whether an organization is actively and openly cultivating engagement or not, employees can use the steps in the following chapters to amp up their performance and results. More importantly, employees can start dictating their future, rather than waiting for someone else to determine their level of success .

Along the way, we will enjoy more real-world examples from employees (or their employers) who have explored these techniques or strategies, and what they experienced when using them. We will uncover how engagement is a much more empowering and healthy approach to the workplace and personal career.

It is an innovative approach, putting a large measure of responsibility back in control of the employees.

NOTE: If you are an employee who has picked up this book and opened directly to this chapter, it may be of great benefit to read the leadership chapters, too. This will paint the fullest portrait possible and show you how your actions will create even stronger outcomes.

# CHAPTER 17

## YOU ARE IN CONTROL

So, at the end of all the discussions and studies about employee engagement—what it is, what it does, what it can do, and so on—we have to look at it as coming down to one essential "thing," the most important part of the process, and that is you, the employee.

Engagement on the employee end is not about how to increase the bottom line, or enhance the customer experience, but instead about emotional connection. It is about how to find or regain passion for their job, how to feel that what they do matters, that they are part of a team, and that they are a significant part of their company's success. Once that is in place, the rest will come, and come in a far bigger return on investment than expected.

### THE EMPLOYEE COMPANIES STRIVE TO KEEP

In today's market, everyone seems to be worried: worried about finding a job, worried about keeping a job, and worried about how to get ahead in an already overcrowded market. Unemployment and underemployment rates are at an all-time high, more new businesses are failing, and the economic outlook changes so often that to call it uncertain seems like an understatement.

Sounds depressing! Well, actually it is not. When you look closely, it is not that companies aren't hiring, it isn't that they aren't promoting, and it isn't that they are not working hard to retain employees. These companies just know that in competitive environments, they need the best people on their team if they are going to succeed.

It is just that clear, as an employee you have a choice to make. In these uncertain times, if make the choice to engage you then put yourself in control, you enter the driver's seat, because whether or not you find a job, keep a job, or excel at a job really is up to you. Only you can decide whether you want to engage or not. To engage, you do not need the right leader or the right culture, and you certainly do not need permission to do it. You just simply need to make a choice.

## THE REAL WORLD

## THE CHOICE IS YOURS

*At the age of 17, Adam Tartt needed a part-time job that paid more than he currently had. He was approached by the father of his then-girlfriend, who owned, ironically, a company that created plaques and recognition programs to help their clients engage employees.*

*Adam was hired to work after school in the production department. Raised with a strong work ethic and wanting to hold on to this job, Adam put in the extra effort and did what he was asked to do—and then some—to ensure he and the department excelled in their performance and roles.*

*At the time, the company was small, with just five or six employees, but things were moving fast, and with a dynamic leader, David Long, the company was clearly in growth mode. The more* the company grew, the more opportunity Adam saw, and despite carrying a full load now at college, he went after and asked for any and all additional responsibilities he could take on.

Within a year, personal problems had caused a key team member to leave, and Davidturned to Adam to step in to fill the void. He turned to Adam, despite his age and lack of experience, because Adam had proven (through his actions) that he could be counted on and trusted, and that he was clearly aligned with the values and the vision that David had to take the company forward.

The more Adam engaged the more comfortable David became giving him more opportunity. Adam sought out projects or work he could take off of David's plate, asked for feedback and input to develop his skills and deepen his experience, and did whatever it took—working nights and weekends when the job needed more attention—to make sure things were done on time and done right. Adam treated this company as if it were his own.

Yes, David Long led in a way that ensured Adam was working in a culture that allowed for full engagement, but Adam also shared, and shared in a big way, in what it took to make the culture and the company vision succeed. Adam make a choice to engage, and the return on investment of hard work, initiative, and the right attitude is still paying dividends

Today, Adam Tartt is the company's Chief Operating Officer, second in command at MyEmployees.com, and is the clear successor to David Long. By choosing to engage, by not waiting for the timing to be right, for the leader to suggest, or for the culture to be the right fit, Adam simply chose to grab hold of his own career and chart his own course. Because of his own initiative, Adam is living in the community he wants to live in, is working with an amazing team he helped build, is a leader in a purpose-driven company, and is reaping the rewards of making the choice to become the employee *that companies strive to keep.*

*Today's market may be tough, but understand you are in control. By becoming the employee that today's businesses strive to keep, you'll become the one driving your career and your future!*

## ENGAGEMENT IS NOT DONE TO YOU

It is always surprising to me that few employees recognize that the true benefit of employee engagement is really theirs. Yes, with an engaged team, a company may be more successful, the bottom line stronger, the productivity and efficiency on an upward trajectory, but at the end of the day, there is nothing in life like knowing you are in control of your own destiny.

## REALLY...YOU ARE IN CONTROL!

In the first part of this book, we uncovered a few of these benefits, such as an enhanced sense of well-being, happiness, purpose, more success, and so on. We also looked at the ways in which lack of engagement costs businesses; the steps taken to engage employees; and how leadership can step up and help employees become engaged. But there is actually quite a bit more to choosing to engage than that.

In fact, the employee who embraces engagement, whether the culture presents it or not, is going to become someone who never has to wait for someone else to open a door, provide opportunity, remove the obstacles, or decide their level of success. The employee who embraces engagement will be the most sought-after one on the market.

In today's economy, engaged employees are in the driver's seat, calling the shots, and are of true value to their team members and their leaders. The most engaged employees are going to discover job security at a level they may have never before encountered. They will have careers that are rich and full (no matter what industry or field), and they will get every possible advantage from the initiative they take. And in doing so, will personally determine their level of success.

Business in the Community (a UK organization) lists more than five employee benefits for those employees who embrace engagement initiatives, including:

▸ More opportunity – Being cited as someone who has a great attitude and great skills will lead leaders and organizations to seek you out for career opportunities.

▸ Boosting self-confidence and enthusiasm – knowing you have what it takes to handle any opportunity

▸ Enjoying a much wider range of training or learning opportunities (boosting their chances for career growth)

▸ Building relationships with peers and colleagues, making a strong network that can open doors and uncover opportunities.

▸ Peer support & mentorship – Others seek out and collaborate with engaged employees, providing others to brainstorm with, learn from, and collaborate with on projects or goals.

The most amazing part of any of this is that obtaining it, reaching these levels, and reaping the rewards is all up to you. It truly is a choice.

## A ROAD MAP TO SUCCESS

Employees participating fully in engagement initiatives will enjoy knowing that they are an engine behind their team and their organizations success. And with the engagement initiative being a 50/50 endeavor, it means leaders are just as engaged as employees, taking full note of those who can be called upon to take ownership, step on the path to leadership, and more.

As writer John Schwartz says, "While the Friday afternoon pizza party always breeds goodwill, an engaged leader goes beyond to make sure employees are heard and valued."

## LACK OF ENGAGEMENT IS NOT AN OPTION

What if you are working in an organization without any engagement programs available? What if there is no leader there ready to step the plate and communicate, create, and support an engagement culture?

In reality, whether the support is there or not, you still get to choose to engage. Recall that the definition of engagement (on the employee end) includes "wanting to be passionate about what you do, give purpose to your role, and know full well that the work you do is key to your company's overall success."

Any employee can take steps to achieve such ends. Yes, I will admit that coming to work each day may be tough if there is no culture of trust, support, or encouragement, but it does not mean that is the end of engagement. And honestly, if you want reap the rewards of engagement, you need to choose to engage whether someone is creating the culture or not.

Being engaged, in spite of challenges, becomes its own reward. Yes, it will certainly be much more difficult for the employee in such a scenario, but it does yield some immediate results. For example, the employee who is striving to be as fully engaged as possible—without any company initiative or support—will be proactive to:

▸ Take steps to fully understand their role, and how they can best contribute to the company's success.

▸ Energize their determination on a daily basis, striving to meet the responsibilities of their role.

▸ Look at how they can expand upon their role in leading the company towards success.

- ▶ Communicate to the best of their ability, and take responsibility for the lack of communication and work on their role to improve.

- ▶ Seek growth by investing in and developing others.

- ▶ Own every aspect of their work, take responsibility for failure, and share success.

- ▶ Hold themselves accountable, even if no one else does.

Employees "in the know" about engagement can turn it on its head or reverse engineer it by taking responsibility for it. The power of choosing to engage is within your power, and as an employee, it fuels your professional growth and success. Whether formal programs exist or not, the opportunities are always there.

In other words, if an employer or leader is going to implement a strategy meant to build trust, a well-informed employee will engage with whatever tactics are being used, and gain the comforts and security that come from aligning themselves with leadership. The employee who chooses to engage will work to be more open, honest, accountable, and trustworthy. If an employer is not using any such strategy, the same employee can engage in a strategy of their own to create identical outcomes.

The lesson is you don't have to wait on leadership to engage you , take responsibility to engage yourself. When you do, you will have taken a step in shifting your paradigm to understand that responsibility is not a burden; it is the path to personal power, freedom, and purpose!

## CALL TO ACTION

1. *Your Responsibility – Understand that employee engagement is of most benefit to you the employee. Choosing to engage will do more to benefit you then it will to benefit your company.*

2. *This Is Not A Myth—Your career, your future is directly tied to the choices you make. It is not the company, not the leaders, who will determine your future, it is you.*

3. *Take Control - Now it is your turn, to chart your course, decide your path, and create your strategy as to when, where, how and to what level you are going to engage.*

4. *Don't Wait on Leadership – Quit waiting for someone to share the vision of your company, ask you where you want to be in five years, or explain the best strategies to achieve your goals. Quit waiting on the perfect leader to show you how to engage.*

*Now - If you step up to the plate now and begin using this information to grow your career, you need never fear losing a job, ending up at a dead end, or feeling bored by the work you do. Instead, if you get to work now, you can learn how to use engagement opportunities (whether they exist or not in your company) to drive results and your career. When you do, you put yourself in control of your career and your life!*

# CHAPTER 18

## BECOMING THE EMPLOYEE THAT COMPANIES STRIVE TO KEEP

t is an interesting time, moving out of push economy into a pull economy that puts both consumers and employees in the position of control. Globalization, advancement in technology, and increased competition have created more opportunities for engaged employees to call the shots and choose where, when, how, and for whom they work.

As an engaged employee, you call the shots, and you are in demand. Think about that, If your company is not providing what you need, you can move on and find another opportunity. When we were looking at the new economy earlier in this book, we noted how so many people will actively seek a new job in the coming year—more than 40% of people in some categories.

According to one recent report, "the latest survey of CFOs shows that 72% of respondents did not reduce their workforce over the past 12 months, and 61% of them plan to hire within the next six months. That means employees, those that are engaged employees have more options."

If you are an employee who is happy to sit around and wait for the employer to engage you, then you may be an employee who is waiting a very long time. It is amazing to me they very  people who never see opportunity, are also the ones who never realize they are doing nothing to create it. Waiting on others, especially leaders, to do the work for you, guarantees you will always be in a position of need rather than power.

As a disengaged employee, you may feel that leadership is weak, inept, or disconnected, but even if you are right, I want to ask you, before you point fingers to ask yourself what steps are you taking to connect with? What have you done to become a leader? If your answer is nothing, then remember this is not holding up the 50/50 model for engagement, is it? If your expecting your  employer to engage you, then in all honesty, you are not worth engaging.

Even in a challenging employment climate, leaders learn they can live without you if you are unmotivated and waiting for them to engage you.

So, employees, whether you want to keep the job you have or not, you need to take it upon yourself to fully engage. In today's economy, there is no "fat" in the margin, meaning employers cannot carry dead weight. In today's economy competition is too steep, technology costs too high, and the battle for customers too fierce. As an employee you need to know if you did not engage at your last job, employers understand that the chances are pretty good you are not going to engage at another.

## ACTIONS SPEAK LOUDER THAN WORDS

The engaged employee, the one who gets to call the shots in their career and life, is the one who engages no matter the environment, the culture, or the leader. The level to which you engage when the chips are down says volumes about the level you will contribute and the difference you will make when the culture, the company, and the leader are right. Your actions speak far louder than your words.

How do you become the employee that your company strives to keep? You take charge.

## NO WAITING AROUND!

Take a moment to consider one major truth that sits directly in front of you.

What is it? You are, at this very moment, reading a book that helps employers to engage their employees, and employees to engage in their work. Engage in a way that is a much greater degree of engagement than they currently have or even can imagine. The key to achieving what this book is laying out is you taking action.

Engagement is something that requires action, and therein lays the difference between leaders who create cultures where engagement can thrive, and those who do not. Action is the difference between the employee who waits to be engaged, and the one who engages.

Right now, your boss or your leader may be working hard at figuring out the whole engagement issue, and instead of sitting around waiting for them to present you with answers; you could be driving your own career (and the company) towards success instead.

## THE REAL WORLD

## GRABBING THE BULL BY THE HORNS

*These are the words of Andre Robinson, the head of Advisory Services for Voya Financial Advisors, a top broker-dealer with over 2,200 affiliated financial advisors and a focus on helping advance the retirement readiness and financial security needs of Americans:*

*I am, by all accounts, not supposed to be the success, or in the position that I am today. I mean, think about it: I am fifteen years younger than most other leaders, I am African American, and the path I took to get here was not to say, well, traditional.*

## IN THEIR OWN WORDS...

"There's always something new to learn, and the more skills and knowledge you bring to your job, the more valuable you are as an employee. Take advantage of any training opportunities. If your company offers tuition reimbursement, take classes that enhance your skills, or work toward a degree. Attend any relevant conferences or seminars and keep up with industry trends by reading trade publications and joining associations. Volunteer to learn new tasks or cross-train with another employee or department so you're available to help out as needed."

- (Christensen, 2015)

*For me, if I would have waited for my leaders to come to me, for someone else to decide on and create my career, I believe I would still be waiting. Sure, I had obstacles, challenges, and plenty of stumbling blocks, but I made the decision long ago, that how far I went and what I achieved was up to me. It was me who found my first mentor and who raised my hand for opportunities that came my way.*

*I learned early on that you give off a vibe in the workplace, and if you want to be tapped, if you want to be noticed, you need to make become the person leadership wants to hire before they even think about hiring you. I have been passed over in the past, not based on my performance, but because I was not making sure that I stood out. And I did not wait for anyone to tell me that, coach me on that, I figured it out on my own. If you are performing, and not advancing, take responsibility, and learn to become the employee that you would want working for you. Don't wait for someone else to tell you what to do, take action.*

*Your career and how far you go is really up to you, I am living proof. The only thing holding me back, was me, and what I got out of my own way, my career took off. And because I was running the show, I have advanced farther and faster than I could of if I was waiting for others to advance me.*

## WHAT'S HOLDING YOU BACK?

It is most likely that you have become complacent, used to an inefficient paradigm or model, and need to learn and then implement a new one. That is not as frightening as it sounds, and you may even be more than ready to do so when you discover the flaws of the "waiting around" syndrome.

Have you heard of the term "learned helplessness"? It is applied to employees who have suffered at the hands of overbearing managers, or micromanagers.

Unfortunately, micromanaging is a product of many different factors and can be born out of a manager's worries over being disconnected. It can be due to a leader who would have preferred to remain in a different (previous) role; it can be due to simple pressures to perform and succeed. It can also be related directly to fear of failure.

And, in all cases, a micromanager is one who looks over your shoulder, literally and figuratively, watching every little thing you do. Too many modern employees have experienced something like this scenario, and believe that they have little to no control over it. And feeling out of control, they complain about it. Again, maybe justified, but a complete waste of time.

The problem with complaining, despite the fact that it is fun, is that it turns you into a victim, and once you become a victim, that is all you are ever going to be. The moment you become a victim is the moment you make the fatal decision to spend more time and energy focused on those things over which you have little to no control, and you lose the energy you need to focus on those things you can. Those very things that will move you forward, and put you in control of your own career.

So rather than becoming a victim, take the steps you need to take to become the employee that companies strive to keep.

## STEPS TO FULL ENGAGEMENT

▸ Take ownership - Your job is yours, so act like the company, and the success of it is yours too. Start treating clients, colleagues, responsibilities, and outcomes as if you actually owned or had a stake in the company. Modern businesses know that the new economy is more than just competitive, and to succeed in it, they need the top people. Do what it takes to make things happen by taking full ownership of your work and responsibility for the company's success.

▸ Look at your attitude – Attitude is everything, and the great part is that it is something over which you have total control. You can choose to be positive, choose to be optimistic, and choose to fully engage.

▸ Connect - If you want your work to be about something more or to have purpose, make sure that one of the most important purposes is the people you work with and for. In other words, make it your job to connect and build relationships proactively. These relationships should be with colleagues and peers (within and outside of the firm), clients (even if it is just providing helpful and patient service), and all others you interact with. Relationships and connections grow a career and if you build your network, and you will change your life.

Taking ownership with an attitude in line with company goals, and using your daily work to connect with others and drive the organization towards success; now, that is the kind of employee who companies strive to keep.

It is also an accurate description of an employee who is fully engaged. After all, it would be impossible to do such things without engagement!

## IN THEIR OWN WORDS...

"It might not seem fair, but quietly efficient employees don't always stand out enough to be deemed indispensable. A formal or informal mentor in your workplace can offer valuable advice and expand your network within a company. If you're senior enough, offer your services as a mentor to new employees. If you're taking advantage of training or further education, provide progress reports to your supervisor. Volunteer to help organize company events, write articles for a company newsletter or serve on committees to increase your visibility."

- (Christensen, 2015)

## CALL TO ACTION

*While you will want to become an engaged employee to enjoy the many benefits we considered in the previous chapter, you also want to engage because it proves you to be an invaluable employee to your company—the kind they will work hard to keep on board. So ask yourself:*

1. *How much ownership have I taken?*

   *In other words, have I defined my role rather than waiting for my boss to do it? Have I asked all of the relevant questions, discovered where the company is headed, and where I fit into that? Have I asked about what it is that I can do to ensure the company's success? Am I going beyond the basic to-do list and using my energy and creativity to make the work my own?*

2. *Am I taking responsibly for my own success?*

   *Or am I waiting for someone else to do it? Engaging is not about waiting for a leader to ask or a culture to be created. None of those things need to be in place; the choice of engagement and success are up to you.*

3. *What about my attitude?*

   *Am I positive, and do I create good energy? What is the impact I have on colleagues and peers? What can I do to ensure that I am grateful for any and all opportunities that I have? What can I do to make myself the kind of person others in the workplace want to be around?*

4. *Am I connected or disconnected?*

   *Am I taking responsibility to connect to my peers, leaders, and the company's vision and mission? Am I working to build my network, expand my center of influence, and build relationships that matter?*

# CHAPTER 20

## ATTITUDE: IT'S A CHOICE

A ttitude is arguably one of the most important attributes in success, and certainly one that employers look to when determining who to hire, who to promote, and who to keep on board. The great thing about attitude is that you are one hundred percent in control of yours. Think about that: one of the strongest attributes in determining your success, and you have one-hundred percent control over it!

### THE REAL WORLD

*When I think about attitude and the power of it, I think about Katie O'Brien. Katie is the executive assistant to the executive partner of Horne LLP, a company we have introduced and spoken about extensively in this book, a company that is the very example of a culture of employee engagement.*

*Katie's story was one of the first things that caught my attention with Horne, and one of the reasons why I knew their leadership and their firm was different. When I met Katie, I noticed immediately she was upbeat, funny, positive, and passionate about her company. I also noticed she was young. I discovered soon afterwards that* though she had not been with HORNE very long, she held this prestigious and important role.

I was intrigued, so I was anxious to learn her story. She shared with me that she had previously worked as the receptionist at the company whose lobby sits on the ground floor of the building where HORNE has its corporate headquarters. It was her job there to answer the phone, direct the calls, and greet clients. She took it all, and then some, very seriously, and from day one decided to treat people as if they were coming to her home.

Katie took the extra step to learn names, recognize voices, learn personal things about them, and go above and beyond to ensure they got what they needed. As one would expect of any engaged employee, she did this with clients and co-workers alike. However, Katie did not stop there. She made up her mind that if she were treating people like this was her home, she should greet everybody, whether they were coming to her place of business or not.

So that is what she did: While not her job, and definitely not expected of her, she began greeting everyone who came through the doors of "her" building—greeting them by name, with a big smile, and doing any and all she could to help them. Unbeknownst to her, one of the people she greeted every day with a big smile and infectious attitude was Joey Havens, the executive partner of Horne LLP. Katie had no idea who he was, where he worked, or what he did; she just treated him like she did everyone else, as if he was coming to her home. And although he never visited her company, and it was not her job to greet him, she still did, with the same great attitude she gave everyone else.

When Joey Havens, executive partner of HORNE, needed to hire a new executive assistant, he contacted Katie O'Brien. No one was more shocked than Katie.

One day Katie was sitting at her desk, greeting people as she *always did, when the Human Resources director from HORNE called and asked if she would be interested in interviewing for a job. Now, I have not shared with you that up until this point, Katie was not necessarily happy at her current job. She was bored, and despite taking every opportunity to do and take on more, the company was not doing anything to move her up or expand her position.*

*So when HORNE called, even though Katie was a little scared she was not qualified for this job, she still responded with a yes. The rest is history, and that is how a young office worker with a strong work ethic and a great attitude landed a promising career with an amazing company. That is the power of attitude and the power of engaging, whether your company recognizes it or not—you never know who is watching or what opportunity is around the corner.*

*Yes, Katie was right—there were better-qualified applicants that wanted that position, but none had a better attitude, and none were fully engaged whether conditions rewarded it or not.*

*Your attitude, just like your career, is truly in your hands and in your control. This is important, because it shows that anyone finding themselves in a negative environment can still choose a positive attitude. If you feel like the underdog, overwhelmed, without much support, your attitude can provide you with a surprising amount of energy and benefit. Yes, attitude is always a choice, and choosing to have a great one puts you in a much better position to become the employee that companies strive to hire and to keep.*

---

## WHY ATTITUDE MATTERS

If Katie's story is not enough to convince you, here are a few other reasons that attitude matters and is a key driver in determining your level of success.

According to Keith Harrel, one of the most important steps you can take toward achieving your greatest potential in life is to learn to monitor your attitude and its impact on your work performance, relationships, and everyone around you (http://www.success.com/article/ why-your-attitude-is-everything).

Anyone can learn the same skills, get the same education, and study the things that you do, but what separates you from your competition is attitude. Companies can train you to do just about anything, but they can't teach you attitude. Why? Because attitude is a choice, one over which you have total control.

## CHOOSING THE RIGHT ATTITUDE

See the glass as half full

The right attitude starts with perception and choosing to see what is right in the workplace, rather than what is wrong. That is easier when you start your day thinking about those things for which you are grateful. Every day find three things to be grateful for at work; write them down or say them aloud. Either way, keep them front and center. Set your mind right and your attitude will follow.

## CHOOSE YOUR PERCEPTION

You can take two different people from the same exact situation, and each of them chooses to see things from a totally different perspective. Your perception, how you choose to view things, determines your attitude. Notice the people you work with. Some will say they love Mondays, while others come through the door complaining. So what is your perception? What is your paradigm?

After a workshop I had done in Washington, DC on networking, I headed out with four attendees to go to a networking event, to put their new found skills into practice. We quickly got lost, all five of us trying to find this networking event. After searching for an hour, we finally found the right street and started following building numbers to find the correct address. However, that proved difficult: It was dark, every building looked empty, and we were struggling to both see and find the right numbers.

One of the guys with us, Paul, just started immediately complaining, moaning things like, "This is not right; we are lost; this is just another wild goose chase; we are going to be out here all night; we will never find it." We were all sick of listening to him, when one of the women, Susan, piped up and said, "Maybe it is a networking event that is being held by candlelight." We all immediately broke out laughing and thought, "Wow, who cares if we ever find this place—she is making this so much fun." And it caused me to think about her—the truth was, she was always fun, always upbeat and positive, and always the type of person who saw the glass half full. Because of that attitude and that perception, she is someone I would choose to be around, and Paul, well, he is not. Sure enough, we found the building and made it to the event. But getting there with Susan was so much better than getting there with Paul.

## IN THEIR OWN WORDS…

"Attitude, to me, is more important than education, than money, than circumstances, than failures, than successes, than what other people think or say or do. It is more important than appearance, giftedness or skill. It will make or break a company… a church… a home. The remarkable thing is we have a choice every day regarding the attitude we embrace for that day. We cannot change our past… we cannot change the fact that people act in a certain way. We cannot change the inevitable. The only thing we can do is play on the one string we have, and that is our attitude… I am convinced that life is 10 percent what happens to me and 90 percent how I react to it. And so it is with you… We are in charge of our attitudes."

- (Maxwell, 2014)

## SMILE & LAUGH

Choose to approach each day with a smile, and make the time to laugh. This isn't rocket science, people want to be around people who are upbeat, positive, and fun. People are drawn to the positive, and humor is engaging and attractive. Attitude is a choice: Choose to be grateful, to see the glass half full, and to smile and put a little fun into the workplace.

Put a smile on your face. Do it now! Do you feel your energy change? Do you feel your mood lift? Well what you experience when you smile, is what other are experiencing about you too. Think about what you bring the workplace, to the client's office, and then choose to bring a smile and a laugh rather than a somber face and a complaint about the weather or your workload.

Research is proving that in a challenging economy, attitude is one of the top qualities employers look for when hiring or retaining employees. The key, as we have all heard many times, is to realize it is not what happens to you that matters; it is how you choose to respond.

Here are my six tips for grabbing hold and learning to control your attitude:

1. Write It Down: Think of the attitude you want to have, the way you would want to be described, and the person you want to bring into the workplace each and every day. Write it down! If you want to control your attitude, you need to first determine what you want your attitude to be.

2. Read It: Read it first thing every morning; start your day by making yourself conscious and aware of the attitude you want to bring into the workplace. You have to read it and choose to be it each and every day. I do this every morning—that is how I start my day by "reading and then choosing my attitude." I want to bring that ideal attitude to the workplace and my clients, so I make a mental commitment to do so.

3. Be Conscious - Take a moment before you enter a room, meet with a client, or go to a meeting to think about your attitude and recommit to presenting that attitude you wrote down. For example, if want to be someone who is upbeat and positive, then you need to recommit throughout the day to be that.

4. Choose Wisely: Your words, actions, and tone all reflect your attitude. Make sure they align with who you want the world to see.

5. Make Room: Make room to re-energize! Keeping up a great attitude can be hard, especially when not everyone around you is doing the same. Make room and time in your day to reinvest in yourself, to keep your energy and your motivation where they need to be.

6. Take Control - You can and must always choose to bring the best you, the best attitude, into the work place.

Remember that part becoming an employee that a company wants to keep is building relationships, internal and external to your company. If you do not choose a positive attitude each time you enter the front door, you are unlikely to be the person others want to be around, and the one with whom others want to build a relationship.

Making excuses for a poor attitude—one day it is the weather, one day it is a headache, another day it is "just because"—makes you unpredictable, and unpredictable people never gain the trust of those around them. Trust is crucial to stability, success, and growth in the workplace.

You will struggle to build relationships if you do not take control of your attitude. Fail to choose the best attitude, and you will fail to reach your goals. Your talent, skill, and knowledge can only take you so far; after that, it comes down, almost entirely, to your attitude.

## CONSIDER THIS QUOTE FROM <u>ENTREPRENEUR</u>:

The key to beating the competition and achieving success is mental, reflected in one's attitude, totally controlled by the individual. This holds true in most human endeavors besides business. How many times have we seen the underdog team or player win over the more talented opponent? The difference is often attitude.

This means you need to consistently choose an attitude that will bring you such results, and the following behaviors are essential:

▸ Be aware - I like to remind people (both at leadership levels and employees) that it is never what happens to you that matters, but how you react to it, that counts the most. We all have years of mental and emotional programming, and tend to use reactions-based attitudes. You need to de-program yourself and choose your attitude based on workplace or situational needs instead. This makes you predictable, dependable, and consistent.

▸ Choose optimism over pessimism - There are two points (or more) to everything. Choose the optimistic point or angle. That means seeing problems or challenges as opportunities. For example, the task your boss has set before you may be tough, but rather than resenting the difficulty, embrace their trust in you to overcome this problem—it is an opportunity to show them what you can do!

▸ Be passionate about work - Ownership is fueled by passion, and when you are this motivated, you are likely to choose the best (i.e. productive) actions. Engagement programs strive to get people passionate about their work, so take time to discover what it is that fuels your fire for your industry, career, job, and so on. Then, when you are struggling with your attitude, it will be this passion that helps you regain a positive outlook.

▸ Be communicative - This means talking and listening, taking feedback and using it, and doing all that you can to build stronger relationships. When you focus on communication, your attitude automatically becomes much less reactive and far more positive and helpful.

It is not a shock to anyone that your attitude is one of the biggest factors in your success. What can be a bit surprising, however, is that your attitude is totally within your control. You are in control to a degree that few generations of employees have ever been. Engagement programs are like road maps to optimal career growth, and if you have the right attitude, it can take you as far as you determine you want to go—even if your company lacks any engagement programs or clear pathways to leadership or success.

The key is to never sit around and just wait to be engaged or asked to participate.

## CALL TO ACTION

1. *Understand that engagement is your choice; lack of programs, leadership, or culture is never a reason not to have a great attitude, or not to engage.*

2. *Decide what it is that you want, then start to draw a roadmap of what you need to do to get there.*

3. *Choose your attitude; follow the steps and the outlines we created to be positive, upbeat, and someone others want to be around.*

# CHAPTER 21

## PERSONAL LEADERSHIP

W hen you choose to become the employee that companies strive to keep, you actually need to become that type of employee. Just like you want to be associated with a successful company, employers want to be associated with successful employees. Companies know that in order to move forward, take care of their clients, and earn a profit, they have to have the best people on the bus. They need people who care about the customers, people who care about the company and people who are dedicated to helping the company become and remain successful. Leaders need people who come already equipped with ideas, opinions, and drive. They need you to have and take charge of your own personal leadership.

### THE "AUTOMATIC" EMPLOYEE

In writing and researching for a White Paper I developed on the state of employee engagement in the financial services field (go to www.meridithelliottpowell.com to get a copy of the report), I interviewed top executives and CEOs about their views on the challenges they are facing and what they as a company are doing about the issue.

I began each interview by focusing on the individual and asking them about their rise up the corporate ladder, and what or who "engaged" them in their own success. Down to the person, every individual I interviewed said his own personal initiative. Sure, they had mentors, good training, and some good and bad role models, but all agreed it had been their own drive, their willingness to raise their hand, and their own personal leadership that had been the deciding factor as to why they progressed in their careers.

If you are lucky enough to get one great leader in the course of your entire career, then you are "lucky enough." Again, leadership is a choice, a personal choice; it is not something you have to wait for someone to share with you. You can be a great leader without a solid role model, you can be great leader without someone mentoring or asking you do it. It is something, quite frankly, you should care enough to do yourself.

## THE REAL WORLD

### INVEST IN YOURSELF

*David Long, CEO of MyEmployees.com, is committed to the growth and development of the individuals who make up his team, and his team as a whole. He readily gives them opportunity to learn new skills and take courses they have an interest in, and encourages personal growth and development.*

*Among the most popular opportunity is their weekly "book club" meeting. Monthly, David, or a member of his team, chooses a book that they all read, and then schedules a time to discuss it. David buys a copy of the book for every member of his 54-person team, and he creates the time in their schedules and pays them to discuss the book. In addition, David engages and shares in the learning and discussion with them.*

*Hands down, for the majority of the team members at MyEmployees.com, this is one of their favorite "perks," a major benefit to working there. As you might guess, a few team members over the years have struggled with the concept, seeing it more as a burden than a perk—seeing it as something they "have" to do, rather than something they are paid to do that adds to their personal benefit and growth.*

*The result? At that moment David, and the other members of the team, know this person is not a fit. They do not share the values and the vision of the company, the most important of which is to invest in yourself and commit to continually grow and learn.*

*David, a tireless supporter and investor of those who work for him, likes to say, "If I am more interested in your growth and development than you are, then you are not the right fit for our team."*

## LEAD YOURSELF

So that begs the questions: How do you lead yourself? What is personal leadership? If you recall, in earlier chapters we have defined leadership as the skill and ability to inspire and develop others in their personal growth and development, while collectively moving everyone you lead towards a common goal.

Personal leadership, in my opinion, is about grabbing the bull by the horns and not waiting for someone else to do that for you, but making it happen yourself. This quote, which I love, just about sums it up:

Personal leadership is the ability to direct your own life and to lead yourself in the direction that you would like your life to take. It is the ability to define what you want out of life and how you are going to get there. Personal leadership means leading, directing, and taking action. It means taking the time, making the proper effort and finding the correct tools to achieve the goals that you want to achieve. (McGowan, 2013)

So, there is leadership, and there is "personal leadership."

## YOUR LEADERSHIP BRAND

According to Norm Smallwood, co-founder of The RBL Group,, a strategic HR and leadership systems advisory firm, and author of several books on leadership, defining and desiring personal leadership is a good start, but to truly "just own it" you need to go further than that and actually have a leadership brand. And, as is always the case with brand, you actually have one, whether you have created it or not. So understand, it is much better to be on the side of being the person who proactively defines and shapes their own brand.

As Smallwood suggests, "your leadership brand conveys your identity and distinctiveness as a leader" (https://hbr.org/2010/03/define-your-personal-leadership). Your leadership brand tells your team, without you saying a word, the leader you are and the leader you have the ability to be.

Yes, you guessed it, to have the right leadership brand; you need to "choose" what you want it to be, then go about the task of creating and acting on it.

1. What results do you want to achieve in the next year?

   As it relates to your organization, what is it that you want to achieve in the next year, and what impact do you want to make? Smallwood suggests you focus on the following four areas when setting those goals:

   ▸ Customers

   ▸ Investors

   ▸ Team Members

▸ Your Company

2. What do you want to be known for?

   Again, when you think about your team members, the other leaders in your company, and your customers, what is it that you want them to say or think about you? What reputation do you want to have?

3. Define your leadership brand.

   Once you establish what you want to be known for, this step should be easy, and that is to clearly define it. In other words, write it down—make it real. Use statements such as "resourceful and strong work ethic," or perhaps "team player and collaborative."

4. Create your leadership brand statement.

   Nothing is truly real until you write it down, so write yours down and bring it to life.

   I want to be known for _____, so I can deliver_____.

5. Make it real.

   My personal favorite step is to make it real. In short, deliver on the promise. Keep your identify front and center, and be mindful to "be it" each and every day.

## TAKING CHARGE

As I shared at the beginning of this chapter, if you find one great leader to work for in your career, you should consider yourself lucky. I don't think I have to tell anyone reading this book how hard it is to find great leaders, in our workspace and in our lives.

So that begs the question, "If there is a leadership void, if most associates would say that the leadership that work for them is lacking, then why would you ever entrust every aspect of your career and/or your future to someone else?" Great leadership or not, no one knows better than you do what you want, what talents you have, and what to do to make your vision become a reality.

Leading yourself is about taking charge and making things happen. To do that, you have to make the decision to get involved and get engaged with your company and your career. To do that, you need to:

## UNDERSTAND YOUR EXPECTATIONS

Too often, we wait for leadership to tell us what to do, to share what is expected of us. Why? If you want to excel at personal leadership, then make it your business to know what is expected of both your position and your department. Ask the questions, learn the goals, and understand how you can best make an impact. In a perfect world, companies and leaders  ensure we understand the company vision, mission, and goals. They make sure we are clear on our priorities and such, but let me be the first to tell you the world, and the working world, are far from perfect. If you want to be the employee that companies strive to keep don't wait for anyone else to tell you, help you, or guide you. Instead, just lead yourself. You make it your mission, your job, to understand what is expected of you and how to "over-deliver."

## RAISE YOUR HAND

Understand that what you do early in your career—the jobs you choose to take, the skills you choose to learn, and the variety of jobs you become exposed to—will have a huge impact on how much you learn, the connections you make, and how far you go in life and in your career.

Personal leadership is about being willing to do the uncomfortable, step to the plate, and raise your hand. As you will soon learn (when you are promoted and excel beyond your wildest dreams), leading an organization is not easy, and you need people at every level willing to take on the jobs that may not be the most exciting at the time. One of the strongest ways to become the employee that companies strive to keep is to Raise Your Hand.

## THE REAL WORLD

### STRATEGIC SACRIFICE

*Chris Madison began his career in public accounting as an intern with HORNE LLP. Unsure of what he wanted to do specifically with his education, he was clear on one thing: He wanted to make a difference and serve both the people he worked with and the clients he worked for. HORNE, the company and the people, aligned perfectly with his value system.*

*Still, even though Chris felt he had landed at the right place, he was uncertain how best to use his talents and his skills. Aligning with the service mentality of the Wise Firm culture at HORNE, he led first with his values, and looked for every opportunity to serve, "raising his hand" to take on jobs and assignments that others did not want to do, that at times did not even appeal to him.*

*"As I look back on it now, it was probably one of the smarter decisions I made, and I do not believe I would be where I am now if I was not willing to put the needs of the company and my team ahead of my own."*

*When describing "what" he did, Chris has come to refer to it as Strategic Sacrifice, making the decision to first invest in your company before you ask your company to invest in you. This meant moving to an office in another state with his new bride for a period of time, leaving family and all that was familiar. It meant learning a new and developing specialty for the firm and teaching others along the way. It meant sacrifice on multiple levels. "It is delayed gratification; I knew the right role and the right opportunity would come along, and I knew, almost instinctively, that I would need to be ready. The best way to be prepared was to learn as much as I could, and the best way to do that was to 'raise my hand.'"*

*Because he took on roles and opportunities that were perhaps not his first choice, he gained skills and knowledge, and a reputation as a someone the firm could count on, who (if called upon to do so) could put the client's and the firm's needs ahead of his own. So naturally, when the right opportunity appeared, Chris was ready both from a skill perspective and a reputation perspective. Yes, he put the client and the firm ahead of his needs for a period of time, making a strategic sacrifice, but in the long run, that sacrifice paid off, landing and helping him discover the role he really wanted, and giving him the reputation that ensured he had the support to get it.*

## SOLUTION-ORIENTED

Leaders are problem solvers; those who embrace personal leadership become problem-solvers who make leaders aware of complications while presenting solutions. Today's economy is about change—we have established that. With change comes challenges, roadblocks, and obstacles; waiting for someone else to solve or remove them puts your future in others' hands, the one place you do not want it to be.

Just imagine: You're the boss, sitting in your office with more on your to-do list than you can ever hope to get done. Just then, two employees knock on your door, both with the same problem. The first employee spends ten minutes complaining to you about the situation about how no one will do what they're supposed to do and how it is messing up their job. Then they stare at you (again, the boss), expecting you to do something. The second employee comes into your office and spends thirty seconds telling you the problem. Then they spend the next five minutes saying what they think could be done to solve the problem, with the actions they want to take to get that going. If push comes to shove, which employee would you strive to keep? Yes, personal leadership is about being solution-oriented.

## REWARDS & RECOGNITION

When it comes to engaging employees, rewards and recognition always play a part. When we think about reward and recognition, we typically think of who is giving them to us, but when you take on the role of personal leadership, you change your focus from rewards and recognition to others. You give the rewards and you spread the accolades to others. Yes, I realize that sounds counterintuitive to get others recognized when you are trying to keep your job or get promoted. But believe me, leadership notices far more those people who are able to give or share the credit with others than those who constantly toot their own horn. Showering the rewards and appreciation on others not only ensures they are recognized and noticed for what they do, but helps executive leadership see you in a role as a future leader, as someone who can recognize talent and develop it. You become knowns as some who can  motivate and inspire others. If you want to be the employee companies strive to keep, then reward others for their behaviors and results.

## THE BENEFITS OF PERSONAL LEADERSHIP

What would you say if someone offered you a roadmap to success? If they said you could be given a plan or set of steps that could take you along a very sure path to the career goals you craved? Naturally, you would say, "Yes, please!"

Fortunately, personal leadership is a reliable way to receive this sort of map; it helps you to recognize opportunities, make the kinds of plans that will take you closer to your goals each day, and gain the kind of recognition you need and deserve.

It does this by helping you:

▸ Develop talents and skills

▸ Earn recognition

▸ Gain visibility

▸ Identify mentors

▸ Recruit support and help to advance others

You are not going to be sitting around waiting for leadership to lead. You are going to be tapping into your personal leadership. You will be keeping a sharp eye out for opportunities of all kinds and recognizing how they integrate with goals. Your attitude converts hurdles and challenges into learning opportunities, as well.

Of course, first you need to know just what it is that your leadership is seeking to gain. Thus, one of the primary benefits from personal leadership is having a clearly defined mission, vision, or purpose. So many of us go through our entire lives lacking clarity of mission or purpose, and to have this is an invaluable strength.

Having a mission and following through on it is tough, but personal leadership helps build on your existing strengths, and puts to use every experience. In the wise words of author Randy Pausch, "Experience is what you get when you didn't get what you wanted."

Your role as a personal leader is to capitalize on those experiences. It takes commitment, but leadership of any kind is only possible through your commitment and your action. If you take ownership of your personal leadership, it will not only give you a feeling of peace and control, but it will inevitably bring you to the attention of company leadership—those who can move your career forward.

## IN THEIR OWN WORDS...

"Control is not leadership; management is not leadership; leadership is leadership. If you seek to lead, invest at least 50% of your time in leading yourself—your own purpose, ethics, principles, motivation, conduct."

- (Hock, 2013)

The employee who displays personal leadership traits is one who shows they are coachable to the degree needed to assume greater responsibility at all levels of the organization. They will have persistently displayed interest in gaining or increasing their expertise, and they will also reveal a willingness to be mentored and a desire to learn.

### CALL TO ACTION

*In today's economy, leadership must be present at every level. There is too much change and competition, too many new opportunities and advancements in technology for just one person or even an executive team to be leading the company. Leadership today is everyone's job, and personal leadership is the answer.*

1. *Define who you want to be as a leader and how you want to be described.*

2. *Own that description. Decide right here, right now, in this moment, that you are committing to be and transform into that person.*

3. *Ensure your actions match your words.*

4. *Define what it will take, what you need to get there. Do you need more experience, networking, or relationship building?*

5. *Take inventory of your relationships and your network:*

*List one person in your company who would go to bat for you.*

*List one person in the company who is your advocate, that person who just brags about you all the time.*

*List one person in the company who credits you for their growth and development.*

*List one person in your company who relies on you as a resource.*

*If your list is long, relax—you are in great shape. If not, we have some work to do, and with that, we are ready for the next chapter.*

# CHAPTER 22

## THE VALUE OF CONNECTION

B uild your network, and you will change your life. Those are words I live by, and some of the most important advice I believe you will ever receive as it relates to your career.

The relationships you proactively and strategically build hold the keys to "mastering" the workplace and becoming the employee today's companies strive to keep. The more people you know and are able to help, the more successful you will be. It is a proven fact, all things being equal; background, education, and skill set. Those who are better connected, those who have stronger relationships, are promoted more often, are paid more, get more opportunity, and have higher levels of job satisfaction.

### THE REAL WORLD

*Andre Robinson, head of Advisory Services for Voya Financial Advisors, learned early on the value of relationships, and credits his success to this very strategy. In fact, he believes that the ability to build relationships and the actions he took in creating them are the single biggest difference between his career stalling and taking off.*

*Early on, Andre exceled from a career perspective—a triple threat of amazing skills, talents, and work ethic. Even with all of that, he still was being passed over and not selected for promotions and opportunities. Frustrated, he set his mind to figuring out the problem. It came down to two things: working in a team environment, and building the relationships needed to get the job done effectively, efficiently, and enjoyably.*

*Armed with that knowledge, Andre turned things around, knowing that the talent to get where he wanted to go was not the issue, and that the power of relationships was what was holding him back.*

*"It was an-eye opener and true turning point in my ability to understand leadership and business. Nothing works without relationships, and no level of skill, talent, or work ethic can make up for not having them or an inability to build them. It is a critical skill in business and in life, and one that every person at every level in the organization needs have," he said.*

*Andre first got a mentor and learned the ropes. As he was blessed with an engaging and high-energy personality that was all it took; Andre's ability to build connections and proactively create relationships took off at top speed, as he embraced the power of building relationships.*

*So how do we build solid relationships? How do we make that emotional connection that helps us build trust and add value to the people that we work with? And who do we need relationships with everyone but more importantly you need a relationship strategy.*

## PROACTIVELY BUILDING RELATIONSHIPS

So how do you build relationships? First, you take accountability and ownership for the relationships you want and need to build. You do not wait for others to build relationships with you; you take the bull by the horns and be proactive.

To build relationships, you have to network; you have to push out of your comfort zone and reach out to people you do not know. Sure, at first it may be awkward and a little uncomfortable, but do it anyway. Yes, life is easier if we stay in our shells and only connect and talk with our current tribe, but if you do that, you will never build your network, you will never gain those relationships that will change your life.

Networking, in my opinion, has to be one of the most powerful skills you can learn and develop, with the highest rate of return on investment. In a world where we are more connected than ever, we are craving "human" connection. It is true, we have more ability than we have ever had to stay in touch with people via email, text, social networking, and so on. However, though that type of connection is great, it is not as powerful or impactful as a good old' fashioned in-person conversation. The better connected you are, maintaining both online and in-person relationships, the easier owning and taking charge of your own career is going to be.

What is the first thing you do when you want a new job or get laid off from your current job? You reach out to your network. What is the first thing you do if you need advice or are faced with a problem you cannot solve? You reach out to your network. The bigger your network, the bigger your opportunity and the better the advice.

## THREE STRATEGIES TO BUILD YOUR NETWORK

### Listen

Step one is to listen! We think about networking as talking, when really the value is to be a listener. That is where you begin: by listening. To master the art of building relationships, you have to approach your co-workers and your teammates with a servant's heart, and you must genuinely care about and be interested in the people you work with.

Listening is critical in any relationship we create, because it is how we show people that we care, that we are interested in them, and that they can trust us. In addition, when we listen, we understand the person we are talking to—we get to know them, who they are, and what is important to them.

### Learn

Step two is about learning. In other words, we invest in them before we ask them to invest in us. People always fear networking because they believe it is about them, and they worry about what to say about themselves. Well, guess what? Networking is not about you; it is about getting to know others. You need to become the master of asking great questions and be prepared to learn from those answers. People will tell you everything you need to know when asked. All you have to do is ask great questions and listen. Keep the focus on them, and let them talk. They will tell you everything you need to know: exactly who they are, what they do, what their biggest challenges are, what they need to be successful. In other words, they will tell you exactly the best way to build a relationship with them.

### Leverage

Step three is where most people drop the ball when it comes to building relationships, and why they do not feel that networking has much return on investment (ROI). If you want to build your network, then you need to hold yourself accountable to leveraging it, expanding those relationships you want to build.

A one-time event does not a relationship make, and in order to succeed and take things to the next level, you need to take inventory of those relationships that could add value to your life and career, and continue to let them grow and build. Good thing you listened and learned first, right? Now you have all the information you need to know which relationships hold the most value, and which relationships you would most enjoy building long-term.

Up to this point, relationship building has been all about the others, and now, because you have invested in others, it is time to leverage what you have learned and the relationships you have built.

A strong network can alter the course of your professional career for the better. Both internal and external networking will provide you with a wealth of opportunities to shape your career.

In Winning in the Trust & Value Economy, I actually took this to furthest extent possible when I explained that "in a world that is becoming increasingly disconnected, connections are the new currency, the very thing that research shows we most crave. All things being equal, skills, talent, education, the more people you know, the more people you help, the more successful you will be."

So what is in it for you? What is in it for the employee who invests in building a network?

In a word: everything. That is not an exaggeration—building your network can and will change your life. It does so by:

- Nurturing personal growth
- Securing your position within your organization
- Expanding your thinking and perspective
- Giving and ensuring you have visibility
- Opening doors and opportunities
- Providing security in terms of having people to call and connect with should you need help, a new position, or just need to know how to solve a problem

Connecting, networking, and building relationships are about first putting the focus on the "other," but in so doing, bringing you a much stronger rate of return. You will be listening and learning first—focusing on them unselfishly; considering what it is that you can do to add value to their lives and careers; asking yourself how to add value to the relationship; and ensuring that those who network with you find it to be as beneficial to them as it will be to you.

## IN THEIR OWN WORDS...

President of Executives Network, Molly Wendell, said this about connections: "Some day, some way, you're going to need something from someone. And that something might not even be for you. It might be a favor for a friend, a neighbor, a co-worker, or someone's son or daughter. The more you focus on building relationships, and the more real relationships you have based on that focus, the easier you'll find it to get things done. Are you ready for that someday?

Most people think networking is only important for salespeople and job seekers. I'm here to tell you the ability to build relationships is a lifelong skill that helps you succeed in anything you do. It also helps make you indispensable."

The "how" of connecting is not rocket science; networking or relationship building is mostly about the questions that you ask, not the answers that you give. It is not about self-promotion in the least. Instead, it emphasizes your skills in getting others to open up a bit through thoughtful questioning.

As a result, you receive a tremendous amount of goodwill and important information, and a bond of friendship that studies have noted as one of the most relevant factors in workplace success.

Journalist Steve Crabtree explained in the Gallup Management Journal:

For many employees, at least for many of those in unhealthy workplaces, this feeling might be familiar. There are numerous workplaces in which employee relations are often characterized by utter indifference, or, worse, jealousy, mistrust, and outright animosity. Negative workplace relationships may be a big part of why so many American employees are not engaged with their jobs.

He goes on to explain that technology has created higher demands for employees to rely upon one another, and yet these "interdependent relationships" suffer from the problems that disconnectedness or poor relationships create.

We have explored the issue of trust in previous parts of this book, and learned that it is the fundamental building block for success. Connection demands trust, too, further illustrating that it must be a priority for both leadership and employees.

Fortunately, at the employee end, networking and making connections can often be a solid way to begin establishing trust. The person reaching out will be asking questions, listening, and responding thoughtfully. When you take action, you prove the relationship has value to everyone involved. More than courtesy or friendship, it is a conduit for support.

Yet, further studies undertaken by the GMJ uncovered some additional benefits from a sense of "kinship" in the workplace. Those who felt selflessness in the personalities of their workplace connections were more engaged, and felt that such connections were setting them up for success.

Trusting and supportive relationships from leadership downward enhance the workplace and professional outcomes. As a key benefit of networking, this cannot be ignored. Of course, that leaves the biggest question: Whom do you need to network with?

## THE "WHO" OF CONNECTIONS

After all, you don't want just a random array of peers and contacts whose relationships don't help either of you. The key here is to apply the same clarity you used when developing your personal leadership mission.

The network you build has to be specific and planned. It can be extensive, but it should also be targeted. Yes, targeted but targeted to whom? That all depends on your goals.

When doing the work on personal leadership, you created a mission or set of goals. You determined where your work overlapped with your personal leadership, and you identified the areas to target your efforts. You discovered that almost any experience could provide you with opportunities for growth or development, if you had the right attitude. However, with connections, your approach has to be a bit more proactive.

I like to use the "sphere of influence" image to help illustrate the smartest and most effective approach to connecting. By sphere of influence, I mean the people whose actions or beliefs can be impacted by you or you by them. A more formal definition of the concept is a field or area in which an individual or organization has power to affect events and developments. Your connections won't be targeted with a lopsided agenda, though. Your goal in relationships is never just, "What's in it for me?" or, "What can I gain by connecting with this person?"

Instead, when you think about whom to connect with in order to create a sphere of influence, you want to think about a reciprocal relationship. Try not to get caught up in a one-way perspective when picturing your sphere of influence. It is not limited to those who will be influenced or impacted by your relationships to them, but also includes those who may influence you.

Your sphere of influence and network could be built on different goals—i.e. sales, marketing, development, elements within the organization (networking with the buyers, supply chains, and so on)— and always on an internal and external basis.

As a simple example, you may be involved in some part of your organization's business model. You are tasked with cutting costs, so you start with a look at your supply chain. Would it be useful to be able to interact with others in the same field or industry who have the same knowledge but different model? Would it be beneficial to have connections with your suppliers or even the competition? Is there a benefit for those parties in the supply chain (internal and external) to have access and interaction with you?

To put it into the most basic terms, who might be a good sounding board for ideas? Who among your contacts would provide you with relevant feedback, guidance, or suggestions? What benefit is there in any of your contacts supporting you in your quest? Have you given them this kind of support? Are you a valuable contact?

That is just a basic look at spheres of influence and networking—you have a role that could affect change, but so too might those in your network. Overlapping as you all do, even if just as competitors, there are influences, information, and details that are mutually beneficial. Connecting, building a relationship, and learning from one another will help you make changes.

Remember too that connecting opens your mind, expands your knowledge, and opens doors, as well. There are many instances of external connecting and networking used by people lower on the chain of command to access higher-ranking individuals within their own organizations. This is a sort of "from the outside in" approach. The point is that an employee who wants to gain visibility and secure their position must also use connections to strengthen their standing within their organization.

To determine whom to build relationships with, visualize your spheres of influence. Whom can you support through your influence? Who can help you to grow or advance your career? Who can learn from you, and who can you, in turn, learn from?

Proactively build connections with those (internally and externally) who can work with your goals, keeping in mind that the well-chosen relationships tend to expand on your opportunities, create them, or develop them.

The old saying "It isn't what you know but who you know" does touch directly on your professional relationships.

## SECURITY THROUGH CONNECTEDNESS

How many firms cut out the "go-to" person? That one employee who seems to be familiar with so many aspects of the business, great at their own job, and a friend to all? How many firms "cut" the person proactively building community, the one who brings people together or whom others count on as a resource? Few firms ever think of eliminating such a worker. In fact, it is the opposite, a person of this caliber tends to enjoy many doors opening before them.

However, even if the firm did make the fatal mistake of "cutting" this person, how much would this person care? Truly, those who build connections to their companies—both internal and external—are sought after constantly by others, and could secure another position easily. They are in charge of their own careers.

When you become one of those positive "take-charge" people in the eyes of colleagues, peers, and local-level managers, you also gain that same reputation with your leadership. The employee who does not wait around for leadership but who is accountable, owns their work, and shows they are thinking outside of the box through networking with others within and outside of the organization is an asset.

If you design your network to help you meet your goals, you will gain knowledge, credibility, experience, and relations that ensure you are constantly growing. This level of engagement makes you highly desirable to your employers (and competition, especially if you network externally), so you can create the kind of long-term stability so absent in many parts of the job market. Of course, that leaves one final question: How do you network?

## THE "HOW" OF NETWORKING

Should you use business conferences, daily meetings, social media, or the company's private site to network? Yes. Building your network is not a task; it is a lifestyle.

Clearly, there is no "one size fits all" answer to where your most likely networking opportunities will arise. However, I can tell you that it cannot be about quantity—it needs to be about quality. It is not how many people you can get to follow your Twitter or how many contacts you've made through LinkedIn. The point is to choose your connections in a way that enables everyone to get things done.

The online world is a very chaotic and noisy one; to navigate through it all requires a road map. Fortunately, you have already been building that as you have made your way through these pages.

Taking time to identify everything from areas of your industry, key players, colleagues, and competitors, you should have a much clearer idea of whom to communicate with and where to find them. Whether it is a real-world meeting at a conference or promotional event, or a social media site like Facebook, the goal is to use your insight to build relationships that can create change (remember the sphere of influence idea)—relationships that are real and not just built online or in person, but that are fluid and solid.

You want to be able to leverage your connections to help you meet goals, but you also want to be a problem-solver, idea-provider, and support-builder. Maintaining connections and relationships requires your input; it is a two-way process. You need to keep thinking about adding value, investing in the relationship. So, as you build your network, keep in mind that you will also have to put in the time to do so with many of the people to whom you connect.

## IN THEIR OWN WORDS...

Author Erica Dhawan says this about her concept of connectional intelligence: "The millennial generation has been raised in an age of only hyper-connected activity. This has really allowed the millennial generation to not only be able to be native to new ways of working, to connective capacities, but also to use it in really unique ways to scan and source ideas, to solve problems through disparate networks, to leverage ideas like social media."

That is known as old-fashioned authenticity, and it is the only way to go when it comes to networking. Ask about others; don't waste time telling them about yourself, especially if they reached out to you! As I said in my previous book on the new economy:

I am always impressed by those who take a real interest in me. They are not trying to tell me about themselves, their companies or sell me something; they are investing in getting to know me, believing that if there is an opportunity here it will emerge. They have carefully chosen me (according to their prospect criteria list) as someone to reach out to, and allow the relationship to unfold naturally. This builds trust, and builds a willingness on my part to engage and get involved with this person.

Trust, willingness, and authenticity: These are all terms I have used in this part of the book as well, and they cannot be emphasized enough when you are making connections and building relationships. The best news is that well designed networks always reciprocate. They become a key resource in reaching professional goals, and they reward all who participate in them with authenticity.

## CALL TO ACTION

1. *Embrace the Idea – Embrace the idea that if you build your network, you will change your life. Commit now to enhancing and growing not only your network, but also your leadership skills.*

2. *Create a networking strategy:*

   ▶ *Determine whom, internal to your organization and external to your organization, you truly need to build a relationship with. Who needs to be in your network?*

   ▶ *Commit to finding the time and opportunity to meet and connect with them.*

   ▶ *Connect with no agenda other than to listen and to learn.*

   ▶ *Build relationships for trust first and leverage second, if at all.*

   ▶ *Take inventory of your relationships—who you know and what they know.*

3. *Align with Goals - The best way to accomplish all of this is to make your plans for networking according to your fundamental goals.*

4. *Create a Sphere of Influence - Take some time now to draw out a map or diagram of your spheres of influence. Who does your effort impact? Whose work impacts yours? Find all of the areas of overlap and begin building relationships on those points.*

5. *Ask First - Remember that you will look inside and outside of your organization in order to network most effec-*

*tively. And when you do begin to build those relationships, remember that you succeed best when you pose questions based on ideas like:*

▶ *What can I do to help?*

▶ *What can I offer to this potential connection?*

▶ *What is their ideal connection?*

▶ *What are their goals or targets?*

▶ *Are they competitors? Suppliers? Buyers? Leads?*

▶ *What can I do to follow up or build on this connection?*

6. *Follow the Rules – Remember, too, that there are some standard rules of networking that include:*

▶ *Remain positive at all times.*

▶ *Speak no ill of anyone… ever.*

▶ *Networking is not about you.*

▶ *Be aware, listen, and respond with more questions.*

▶ *Be interesting and interested.*

▶ *Do not use your agenda to build the connection—use your interest in the industry/field/individual.*

▶ *Be responsive and follow up.*

*Building such connections will make you one of the most well informed people on your team. A "go-to" person will always have value, but especially one who consistently gives back, shows passion, and is a thought leader. Remember, build your network, and you will change your life.*

# CONCLUSION

## YOU – CALLING THE SHOTS

Whether leader or employee, you are living in an era of tremendous change. Technology, global shifts, and increased competition have and will continue to impact how we do business, and what we need to be focused on to succeed.

We have gone from a paper world to a mostly digital one in less than twenty years. We have seen the entire global financial structure shake, begin to recover, and cause a groundswell of changes as a result. These changes exist in the world of business, in the world's consumer markets, and in the workplace. We know now that new employees, who include a younger generation known as Millennials, have created the need for an entirely different paradigm for leadership.

Change is the key word; few of us really love the idea of tremendous change, especially in areas such as business. Even when they no longer work, we are still comfortable with our traditions, those strategies we have had in place and those we know how to use and implement. Even though this traditional approach is not "cutting it" in today's marketplace, leaders and employees find it hard to shed them and start anew.

Fortunately, we have gone over some fundamental changes and procedures that can put you in the driver's seat when it comes to change. These are ideas that you as a leader, and an employee can begin to implement immediately, and ones you can expand and grow with.

Even better, the use of the different steps we have explored will allow you to embrace this shifting economy and make it start working for you. Embracing what you have learned in this book, you can ensure these changes mean opportunity instead of obstacles. This ability comes from your newfound level of awareness of the bigger picture of what has happened, why it is happening, and how to work within the context of these changes.

For you, everything is now an opportunity to take charge, grow, and use what you learn to drive your career or your organization towards its goals.

## ENGAGEMENT AS A KEY

Engagement happens when we share the responsibility—both leadership and employee—and see it as an opportunity to work with, rather than at odds with, one another. We are taking responsibility for our part and redefining responsibility in order to see it as a chance for freedom of choice, rather than a burden.

Responsibility is ownership, stepping up to the plate, having skin in the game, not waiting for someone else to talk about it, do it, or make it happen. The power, freedom, and purpose come when you no longer have to wait for someone else to take charge and do it.

Ownership is one of the strongest of these changes, and it sets off a domino effect—those who own their role tend to also begin to behave in ways that benefit themselves, their peers and colleagues, their customers, and their organizations.

Leaders, you now have the power to create the ideal environment for engagement of the "new" workforce. You now understand how to give employees a culture in which they can engage with purpose (something an engaged employee requires), and a culture that makes it easy to tap into their intrinsic motivations to help them fully engage.

If you are the employee who is struggling without leadership, you have learned that, lucky for you, you are your own best leader. You now understand that external leadership is a gift, not one you need to have to succeed. When you assume responsibility for your own career, proactively create connections, and choose to lead yourself, you stop waiting for others to make things happen; you are now in charge of your own career. You are in control.

## INNOVATION AT WORK

The material covered in these pages is innovative, and gives you the power to decrease stress, increase profits, and gain true competitive advantage. However, it is so much more than that; these strategies hold the key to putting community, fun, and creativity back into the workplace. They are about getting outcomes, but doing so in a way that creates ownership at every level and innovation at every turn.

It is time for a new approach. This is a new economy with a new employee, and it is time for a new strategy of how we grow our business and develop people.

The statistics back this up and actually demonstrate the necessity of implementing the methods we have outlined. After all, 70% disengagement to one level or another is no laughing matter. Billions of dollars go down the proverbial drain every year as employers struggle to give employees what they need to commit, roll up their sleeves, and do the best work possible.

It is not working because so many programs have missed the point. It is not about bonuses, recognition, or shallow rewards (i.e. an employee of the month plaque). It is about purpose, challenge, and trust. Modern employees want more responsibility; they want growth potential, and they seek pathways for learning more about whatever it is they do for a living. The crazy thing is they want to work harder for you, but you have to ask, "Am I standing in the way?"

The shift has to happen at both levels, leadership and employees. We have to stop looking to others to fix this problem, and we need put these strategies in motion and take charge of our own careers. It is not about job descriptions and perfect strategy plans—it is about creating ownership and engaging in the success of your organization, no matter your role or technical level of responsibility.

## GETTING STARTED

So what are you waiting for? You have all the information, ideas, and strategies you need. All that is left is to take action, make it happen.

We have laid the groundwork and given you a solid foundation. Now it is up to you—what you do with the information and how you implement it. But get ready, because when you do this, it is going to create some very positive impacts that turn "jobs" into passions, and responsibility into freedom. This new approach to employee engagement allows everyone to own their career, and control their futures. Good luck!

# SOURCES

Deloitte.com. Global Human Capital Trends 2015. http://www2.deloitte. com/global/en/pages/human-capital/articles/introduction-human-capital-trends.html

Forbes.com. The Real Truth About Employee Engagement. 2015. http://www.forbes.com/sites/robertamatuson/2015/01/13/the-real-truth-about-employee-engagement/

Forbes.com. Why Companies Fail To Engage...2014. http://www.forbes. com/sites/joshbersin/2014/03/15/why-companies-fail-to-engage-todays-workforce-the-overwhelmed-employee/

Gallup.com. Five Ways to Improve Employee Engagement Now. 2014. http://www.gallup.com/businessjournal/166667/five-ways-improve-employee-engagement.aspx

Nikoniko.co. A History of Niko Niko Calendars...http://blog.nikoniko. co/post/82951593841/a-history-of-niko-niko-calendars-in-agile

Powell, Meridith Elliott. Winning in the Trust & Value Economy. Global Professional Publishing. 2013

Reiman, Joey. The Story of Purpose. Wiley, 2012.

TD.org. Employee Engagement: An Epic Failure? 2015. https://www. td.org/Publications/Magazines/TD/TD-Archive/2015/03/Employee-Engagement-An-Epic-Failure

APA.org. Self-Efficacy... http://www.apa.org/pi/aids/resources/educa-tion/self-efficacy.aspx

Bain.com. Who's responsible for employee... http://www.bain.com/publications/articles/whos-responsible-for- employee-engagement. aspx

Bersin, Josh. Why the 'Employee Engagement'... https://www.linkedin. com/pulse/20140407153928-131079-why-the-concept-of-employee-engagement-has-to-change

Bersin, Josh. It's time to rethink the...2014. http://www.forbes.com/sites/joshbersin/2014/04/10/its-time-to-rethink-the-employee-en-gagement-issue/

BITC.org.uk. What are the benefits for employees? http://www.bitc.org. uk/programmes/engage/engage-toolkit/employee-community-en-gagement/what-are-benefits-employees

Burns, James MacGregor. Theory of Leadership. 1978

BusinessDictionary.com. What is organizational culture? http://www. businessdictionary.com/definition/organizational-culture.html

Christensen, Maria. How to Be the Employee... http://work.chron.com/employee-company-cant-live-24185.html

Cohen, Wm. Integral Leadership... http://www.archive-ilr.com/ar-chives-2010/2010-10/1010ilrcohen.pdf

CornellHRReview.org. Transformational Leadership... http://www.cor-nellhrreview.org/transformational-leadership-in-the-coming-de-cade-a-response-to-three-major-workplace-trends/

Crabtree, Steve. Getting Personal in the... http://govleaders.org/gal-lup-article-getting-personal.htm

Deloitte.com. Global Human Capital Trends 2015. http://www2.deloitte. com/global/en/pages/human-capital/articles/introduction-hu-man-capital-trends.html

Decision-wise.com. 5 Personal Benefits... https://www.decision-wise.

com/5-personal-benefits-employee-engagement/

employee-driven-innovation.weebly.com. Employee Driven Innovation. http://www.gallup.com/businessjournal/159851/three-strategies-making-employee-engagement-stick.aspx

Entrepreneur.com. 5 Leadership Behaviors... http://www.entrepreneur.com/article/247099

Entrepreneur.com. How to Stop Micromanaging... http://www.entrepreneur.com/article/218028

Entrepreneur.com. Success is all in the... http://www.entrepreneur.com/article/204504

FastCompany.com. 4 Reasons Good Leaders... http://www.fastcompany.com/3034550/the-future-of-work/4-reasons-good-leaders-are-hard-to-find

FastCompany.com. 5 Ways How Leaders... http://www.fastcompany.com/3045432/hit-the-ground-running/5-ways-how-leaders-achieve-genuine-employee-engagement

(Illopis, Glen) Forbes.com. 10 Ways to Inspire Your Team. 2013. http://www.forbes.com/sites/glennllopis/2013/05/06/10-things-inspire-teams-to-optimally-perform/

Forbes.com. Motivating Employees Has Everything...2014. http://www.forbes.com/sites/datafreaks/2014/09/25/motivating-employees-has-almost-nothing-to-do-with-their-attitude-and-almost-everything-to-do-with-feelings-of-ownership/

Forbes.com. Nine Ways to Keep...2013. http://www.forbes.com/sites/forbesleadershipforum/2013/08/20/nine-ways-to-keep-your-companys-most-valuable-asset-its-employees/

Forbes.com. The Real Truth About Employee Engagement. 2015. http://www.forbes.com/sites/robertamatuson/2015/01/13/the-real-truth-about-employee-engagement/

Forbes.com. Who's Driving Innovation...2006. http://www.gallup.com/

businessjournal/24472/whos-driving-innovation-your-company.aspx

Forbes.com. Why Companies Fail To Engage...2014. http://www.forbes.com/sites/joshbersin/2014/03/15/why-companies-fail-to-engage-todays-workforce-the-overwhelmed-employee/

Gallup. State of the American Workplace Report. 2013.

Gallup.com. Three Strategies for Making Employee...2013. http://www.gallup.com/businessjournal/159851/three-strategies-making-employee-engagement-stick.aspx

Gallup.com. Five Ways to Improve Employee Engagement Now. 2014. http://www.gallup.com/businessjournal/166667/five-ways-improve-employee-engagement.aspx

Inc.com. How to Improve Employee... http://www.inc.com/guides/2010/04/employee-retention.html

Investopedia.com. Skin in the Game. http://www.investopedia.com/terms/s/skininthegame.asp#ixzz3gXauvohf

JenniDoyle.com. Transformational Leadership...2015. http://jennidoyle.com/2015/01/30/transformational-leadership/

JohnMaxwell.com. Attitude - It's a choice! http://www.johnmaxwell.com/blog/attitude-its-a-choice

Kelleher, Bob. Dummies.com. Employee Engagement... http://www.dummies.com/how-to/content/employee-engagement-and-innovation.html

Liveperson.com. The key to company innovation... http://www.liveperson.com/connected-customer/posts/key-company-innovation-employee-engagement

Leadership-central.com. Leadership Theories. http://www.leadership-central.com/leadership-theories.html#ixzz3g9KfIaqv

Leadershipnow.com. How the Best Leaders... http://www.leadershipnow.com/CoveyOnTrust.html

Legacee.com. A guide to transformational... https://www.legacee.com/on-transformational-leadership/a-guide-to-transformational-leadership/

LockheedMartin.com. How to Inspire Innovation. http://www.lockheedmartin.com/us/news/speeches/1114-hewson.html

MartinMcGowan.com. Why Personal Leadership...2013. http://martinamcgowan.com/2013/06/why-personal-leadership-is-important/

McLeish, Judy. Maybe the Traditional Approach... http://www.engagementstrategiesonline.com/Maybe-the-Traditional-Approach-to-Engagement-is-All-Wrong/

Merriam-Webster.com. Trust. http://www.merriam-webster.com/dictionary/trust

Nikoniko.co. A History of Niko Niko Calendars...http://blog.nikoniko.co/post/82951593841/a-history-of-niko-niko-calendars-in-agile

OzPrinciple.com. Employee Engagement... https://www.ozprinciple.com/services/employee-engagement/

OzPrinciple.com. The Power of Ownership. https://www.ozprinciple.com/services/employee-engagement/

OzPrinciple.com. Why Accountability. https://www.ozprinciple.com/self/why-accountability/

PeterStark.com. What is your Leadership Role... http://www.peterstark.com/leadership-role-in-employee-engagement/

PeterStark.com. What is Transparent Leadership. http://www.peterstark.com/transparent-leadership-2/

PollyannaPixton.com. Ownership. http://pollyannapixton.com/

Powell, Meridith Elliott. Winning in the Trust & Value Economy. Global Professional Publishing. 2013

PsychologyToday.com. Are you a transformational... https://www.psychologytoday.com/blog/cutting-edge-leadership/200903/are-you-transformational-leader

Reiman, Joey. The Story of Purpose. Wiley, 2012.

Selfgrowth.com. Personal Leadership. http://www.selfgrowth.com/articles/Definition_Leadership.html

SpeedofTrust.com. Organizational Culture Change... http://www.speedoftrust.com/Jobs-to-be-done/culture_transformation

TAICO.com. Discovering and capitalizing... http://www.taico.com/blog/bid/65306/Discovering-and-capitalizing-on-employee-engagement-s-golden-key

TD.org. Employee Engagement: An Epic Failure? 2015. https://www.td.org/Publications/Magazines/TD/TD-Archive/2015/03/Employee-Engagement-An-Epic-Failure

Upenn.edu. How Networking Intelligently... http://knowledge.wharton.upenn.edu/article/power-connectional-intelligence/

ValueOptimismMarketing.com. Workplace Happiness... http://www.valueoptionsmarketing.com/culture/index.php/manager-tools/94-workplace-happiness-what-managers-can-do-to-set-a-positive-tone

Wendell, Molly. How to Build, Influence and Leverage... http://www.welocalize.com/how-to-build-influence-and-leverage-your-network/

WSJ.com. Employees Hold the Key... http://www.wsj.com/articles/SB10001424052748704100604575146083310500518

Powell, Meridith Elliott. Winning in the Trust & Value Economy. Global Professional Publishing. 2013

Reiman, Joey. The Story of Purpose. Wiley, 2012.

Harvard Business Review: Define Your Personal Brand Leadership https://hbr.org/2010/03/define-your-personal-leadershi

TD.org. Employee Engagement: An Epic Failure? 2015. https://www.td.org/Publications/Magazines/TD/TD-Archive/2015/03/Employee-Engagement-An-Epic-Failure

# ABOUT THE AUTHOR

Meridith Elliott Powell

Business Keynote Speaker & Business Growth Expert

Creating Ownership At Every Level; Profits At Every Turn

"Have never seen a presenter go so above and beyond, your energy is amazing and your techniques work. How she got 1200 people up, active and engaged was incredible!"

*Dan Allison, CEO, Vitalize Consulting*

**Meridith Elliott Powell**

**Business Growth Expert**

Meridith Elliott Powell is an award winning business speaker, who motivates her audiences to think big, get active and take action!

With a background that includes corporate leadership positions in banking, finance and healthcare, Meridith has that cutting-edge message, and truly unique approach to the challenges of business growth, employee engagement and the client experience. Meridith helps leaders and organizations create ownership at every level in order to increase profits at every turn.

Known in the industry as a triple-threat, Meridith delivers powerful content, with a lot of energy and a hint of fun, leaving her audiences with a plan of action that ensures they get results and return on investment!

A speaker, coach and author, her book, Winning In The Trust & Value Economy," reveals the strategies of how to make this economy start working for you. This book was nominated for three international book awards, and was named a finalist for the USA BEST BUSINESS BOOK AWARDS. Her fourth book, Own It: Redefining Responsibility powerfully redefines the term personal responsibility and gives the reader proven techniques to inspire their teams to step the plate, take ownership and get passionate about driving results.

Meridith is the host of the Secrets to Success Podcast on the award-winning, international Ambitious Entrepreneur podcast network and is a columnist for several publications, and has been featured in several others including Real Business, American Banker, Investment News, Insurance Today, and American Management. Her innovative webinar series The Client Connection is heard monthly through the BrightTalk Channel and hosts leading experts in the field of business relationships and client service.

> "Powerful content, Amazing presentation; Our clients were fully engaged. Meridith more than delivers!"
>
> *Sheryl Collins, VP, Events, City National Bank*

> "How she can transform from the stage is amazing; I have hired her multiple times!"
>
> *Trish Springfield, SVP, Palmetto Bank*